TOWARD THE HEART OF GOD

TOWARD THE HEART OF GOD

JOURNEY TO CHRISTIAN MATURITY

by

John Dalrymple

WINSTON PRESS

Library of Congress Catalog Card Number: 81-50552
ISBN: 0-86683-602-0 (previously ISBN: 0-232-51428-3)
Printed in the United States of America

5   4   3   2   1

Winston Press
430 Oak Grove
Minneapolis, Minnesota 55403

The longest journey is the journey inward.
Dag Hammarskjöld

The Apostle Paul teaches us to pray everywhere, while our Saviour says: 'Go into your room.' You must not think that he means by this a room with four walls separating you physically from others, but the room that is within you, where your thoughts are shut up, the place that contains your feelings. This room of prayer is with you at all times, wherever you go; it is a secret place and what happens there is witnessed by God alone.   *St Ambrose*

CONTENTS

My thanks are due to Eileen Millar and Charlie Barclay, who gave me valuable criticisms, and to Sister Clare of Jesus, who helped with criticisms, typing and proofreading.

Chapter One

CONVERSION

About thirty years ago I underwent what spiritual writers would describe as a fairly typical religious experience. I was twenty-one years old, had had a conventional Catholic schooling followed by two years' national service in the army and twelve months' hard slogging as a first-year student in the seminary, which I found tough, especially prayer. One day during prayer I all of a sudden underwent the prolonged experience of being unified, simple, collected, at ease before God. The experience, which took place in church – I can name the precise place and time to this day – brought me to birth spiritually. From then on I learnt to pray easily, simply, contemplatively and found that where before it had been hard labour it was now extremely relaxed. The transformation was like beginning to ski down a snow slope after hours of tramping with skis on up a hill. Not only my prayer but the whole of my life began to be changed. The presence of God became 'real' to me in a way that had not happened before. I started to read the Bible and found that passages glowed on the pages as if addressed personally to me by God. I realized, as if for the first time, that he loved me! In the communal life I was leading I found myself undertaking hard tasks which previously I had slid away from or thought myself incapable of. I felt the power of God within me, again as if for the first time. It is not exaggerating to say that my life was filled with an inward ardour from waking in the morning

1

to going to bed at night, an ardour which lasted at least a year. I can remember that the most important discovery was to know that my mediocrity and sins were no obstacle, but even an advantage, to receiving the gracious mercy of God, that pursuing perfection and pleasing God were two quite different aims and that I could do the latter without achieving the former. This so thrilled me that I became somewhat of a prig and a bore explaining this, unsolicited, to my friends. As in all conversions, smugness was not far from the surface. Nevertheless, the experience was real and filled my life with an inward glow of excitement.

This book contains some reflections thirty years after that initiating experience of spiritual simplicity. Looking back, I see that the spiritual expansiveness that followed in the months after the experience was comparatively shallow in the light of later, sometimes painful, deeper experiences. I am grateful for that first experience of exuberant joy which set me alight. I am more grateful for the subsequent modifications of that first joy which have made me dip beneath mere 'experience' to reality itself. These modifications have taken different forms. Some have been deeper versions of the initial experience of one-ness with God in prayer. Others have been experiences in life of public failure or painful humiliations, which have helped me to be less sentimental and more real in my dealings with God. They have all helped me to learn the lesson that the gifts given by our divine Lover are as nothing compared to the Giver himself. In fact letting go of consolations in favour of the Giver of consolations is the lesson we all have to learn sooner or later in spirituality. If we hang about, clutching the consolations of the Holy Spirit to ourselves, possessively revelling in spiritual experiences, we never get started on our journey. This is a pity since it is of all journeys the one most worth embarking upon. It is also, as Dag Hammarskjöld said, the Longest Journey.

Chapter Two

THE MIND OF CHRIST

Issues Today

Anyone who cares about values and standards for living is certain to experience a sense of challenge when looking at today's society. Immense social changes are taking place, and all change, especially social change, challenges people. No one can deny that social change is happening, both in the local society each one of us inhabits and in the wider international society which newspapers, television and radio bring into our homes to have an impact on our local world. Here is an almost random list of 'issues' in modern society: women's lib, gay rights, contraception, euthanasia, minority rights, racialism, colonialism, pacifism, nuclear warfare, the armaments race, peace and justice in the third world, poverty and starvation, alternative lifestyles, ecology, law and order, prison reform, violence, revolution, private schools, women priests. This list of twenty issues, many of which are interconnected but each of which is a distinct question for society to solve, is not just a list of problems which are happening somewhere else and which television merely reports like a football match. They are issues which mankind is involved in as a whole. Clearly in some parts of the world they are more urgent than in others, but there is no country, in the first, second or third worlds, where these issues do not arise. They are indubitably questions for me and my neighbours to answer, not questions which I can stand aside from and leave to others, however strong the temptation to do so.

The temptation to turn one's back on social problems is present in many men and women. If I am honest I confess that faced with most of the issues mentioned above I have a strong urge to opt out, pretend they do not exist, leave them to other people to solve. I may perhaps be concerned that they exist, but I am reluctant to commit myself to having a firm view upon them, still less to doing anything about them. I prefer to let them float free in my mind but not to engage myself upon them to the extent of forming a conclusion, especially a conclusion which might lead to the necessity of action. I can read through a Sunday paper feature on, say, homosexuality and inform myself upon its frequency, its variety and the kind of life homosexuals have to choose for themselves in today's society. At the end of the article I am tempted to pass on to the sports page and leave the problem where I found it as a newspaper feature and no more. My inclination is not to get involved in the problem, not even to the extent of forming a judgement on it. If this is true of issues existing in our country it is even more true of those issues which do not immediately concern us but which matter greatly in other parts of the world. In the list already mentioned, starvation, poverty, peace and justice in the third world are examples. We know about them and can recognize that they are acute problems for a large number of our fellow human beings, but just because they exist outside our own society, away at the other end of the world, we can be apathetic towards them. Because they are not our particular problems, we very easily let them slide out

5

of our minds with the comfortable thought that many people nearer to the problems will be working hard upon solutions.

You do not have to be a Christian to know that this apathy is irresponsible in view of the underlying unity and interconnection of all mankind. But a Christian has an additional reason for being hostile to such apathy, based on the simple truth that we are all children of the one Father and brothers and sisters of Jesus Christ. We know that passing by on the other side of the road is an act condemned by our Master, who gave his life to teach men to care for and be involved in their neighbours. The fact that our neighbour is not only the family next door but also the family starving in Calcutta or deprived of human rights in Russia undoubtedly makes it more difficult for us to be caring. But (unluckily for our native apathy) loving the unseen neighbour is quite as much a Christian duty as loving the one we can see. This especially needs remembering in a world where rich and poor no longer live side by side (as in Jesus' parable about Dives and Lazarus) but live in well separated areas and can pass their whole lives never meeting each other, even though they live in the same city. The unseen neighbour is still a neighbour, though he may live not visibly next door but at the east end of the town or far off in the third world.

The difficulties I have mentioned so far are not new to this generation. It has always been difficult to resolve to care for fellow human beings in trouble. That is the challenge of charity. In our generation to this consciousness of challenge has been added a widespread bewilderment. This bewilderment is caused by the challenge to the mind as well as to the heart which modern issues produce. Quite simply one often does not know what the Christian solution to a problem is. It is not a question of knowing what a solution is and being faced with the personal problem of stirring oneself into action. The problem in this generation is pushed further back. The problem is finding the solution itself to act upon. The difficulty is an intellectual one more than one of execution. Let us turn again to the list of issues on Page 4. Each one is an ethical question mark. For instance, if we think seriously for a few minutes about pacifism, we discover that as Christians we do not readily know what the answer is. Is it right or wrong, optional or compulsory, sense or nonsense? Christian history does not help, because there have been Christian pacifists and Christian soldiers, warrior bishops and Quaker conscientious objectors. Christian theology is equally divided, and in the Gospels themselves quotations can be found to justify both the pacifist viewpoint and the doctrine of the just war. The issue is in fact a thoroughly confusing one. The same consideration can be given to any of the twenty issues in our list, and the same sense of confusion over the lack of a clear Christian answer ensues. What, for instance, is the Christian view on the interconnected problems of violence in the streets, law and order, prison reform? Three Christians sitting to discuss these problems might come up with three distinct solutions, and each might claim to be thinking as a Christian. In fact the puzzling thing about our modern challenge is the large number of issues which are being actively discussed in society, none of which has a proven solution. We could suffer tranquilly being faced with one or two ethical problems which are not clear, but to be surrounded by a society in turmoil which is questioning all possible relationships and institutions is profoundly unsettling. Yet that is the situation today.

7

Change

We live in an age of cultural change. Such ages occur from time to time. Old accepted ways of behaving in society are swept away and new experiments are made. The status quo is challenged. Values are altered. Out of it all comes a new sort of society, initiated by ideas which at first seem outrageously new and by experiments which apply the new ideas and put them to the test of practical living. After that, usually, a settling process begins again, like the Victorian Age which emerged from the new ideas of the French Revolution, or the Elizabethan Era which followed the Reformation in England. We do not know what sort of society is emerging from the present turmoil, though we can guess it will be enormously different from what has preceded it: international rather than national, egalitarian as never before, uniform all over the world, machine-dominated and full of leisure. These are only guesses, because the essence of being in an age of cultural change is not to know what is coming next, only to know that the status quo will not last. We cannot, for instance, tell what the future of family life will be. All we can see is that the old stable form has already disappeared. Relations between husband and wife, children and their parents, even grandparents and the family have all changed due to a conglomerate of new influences from society (women working, nursery schools, old people's homes), medicine (contraception, prolonged life), commerce (teenagers as a separate market for clothes, music and entertainment), the welfare state (social benefits of all kinds). The homes I visited twenty-five years ago as a young priest and the ones I visit in my present parish are strikingly different. I sometimes rub my eyes at the alteration.

Because society changes, the Church changes too. A time of secular cultural change will naturally produce changes in religious culture. Old forms will be abolished, new forms experimented upon and sifted for lasting value. This has happened in the Catholic Church since the Second Vatican Council. I am not qualified to make a professional evaluation of the changes that are taking place in the Catholic Church, but as a member of that Church I can observe the obvious elements in this change of religious culture. Worship has changed from the stylized, beautiful Tridentine Mass to the free and easy people's liturgy of the 1970s. Religious teaching has undergone a similar transition from memorizing fixed formulas to practical, experimental searching. Life in the Church has become more experimental too, and initiatives and movements come up from below more than down from above (which used to be the pattern). Relationships between bishops, priests, people reflect the shift in society at large from distant formality to informal friendship. Participation and consultation are taking over from clerical decrees and obedience.

The medium of change among human beings is questioning. Change begins when someone asks the question: What's the point of doing this; why not do that? If no one asks that question, there is no change; but if enough people ask questions and get together to discuss them, then change is set in motion. In the Catholic Church this questioning of a hitherto unquestioned status quo has been the most notable feature of Catholic life since the Vatican Council. It has been deeply disturbing for some and has resulted in not a few casualties, most obviously among priestly vocations, but also, less visibly, among many lay Catholics who have drifted away from a Church no longer settled. It

9

has given the impression both to insiders and outsiders of an argumentative, not to say quarrelsome, Church. Parish life, in the 1970s, is more talkative and studded with questioning than it was in the tranquil 1950s. All this is merely another way of saying that there is more life than there used to be in the Church. Questioning which leads to change is a sign of life. If the questioning were to come to an end it would be the sign that life was ebbing away. What followed would be settlement, but it would be the settlement of death. Life is unsettling.

There is another form of questioning taking place in the Church which is also a sign of renewed life. This is questioning addressed to society by the Church. A Church which only talked to itself and indulged in internal argument would be only half Christian. So the fact that the Church is now beginning to question the world, society, the state is a significant renewal in Christianity. The Church of South America bravely leads the way, but in Europe the example is being followed, spurred on by memories of the 1930s and 1940s when the Church was ill-equipped to deal with the dictators. This spells the end of the alliance between throne and altar, an alliance deeply embedded in the history of Christendom, but not in fact part of the Gospel message of Jesus Christ. A feature, then, of the religious cultural change we are living through is the championing of human rights by the Church and its readiness to combat secular authorities not to obtain privileges for itself, but for the betterment and humanization of society. We no longer live in a Church which guarantees to be part of the civil establishment, willing to take its place among the stabilizing institutions of society – law, army, police, civil service. In opening itself up to the world after Vatican II, the Church has paradoxically distanced itself from the powers of the world and exercised its right to subvert as well as support the state, depending on what it judges to be necessary. This kind of debate is the more remarkable of the two kinds of questioning which permeate the religious cultural change of our generation.

Coping With Change

What is the average Christian to do when faced with all this change? The temptation is to react with one's guts, that is, to react according to one's temperament, to go ahead with an instant statement and let one's thinking catch up as best it can. This is a very human way of reacting to change and one sees it happening frequently. A quick reaction is forthcoming usually in the form of instant comment, and then the rationalizations follow, but they are rationalizations of a reaction already formed in the instincts and so do not throw much light on the matter. There is very little reason in them. Bishops and priests are not immune from this human tendency. I detect it at work in myself in many parish situations. I react for and against new suggestions with unconsidered speed and only later think up reasons for my reaction. At one level it is human to do this, but at a deeper level it is considerably less than human, because men and women are endowed with minds to form conclusions from evidence submitted, not to produce respectable rationalizations to gloss over their prejudices. We are meant to examine changes objectively and judge them on their merits. The merely emotional reaction is less than human, is immature. In particular it is of little help when we are trying to find what God's will is concerning a particular change.

I suppose there are three instinctive reactions to change. I have already mentioned the first: the desire to run away and make no decision at all. Women priests? We don't know. We wish someone had not brought up the question. We refuse to think about it. We turn our backs on it. We wish it would go away. We instinctively avoid company where this awkward question will arise. We are not available for comment. It is easy to see that this is a cowardly reaction. Clearly it is a temperamental reaction, because you can find no reasonable justification for it, still less a Christian justification. The saints in history have always faced new ideas in the Church, some reacting against novelty (St Bernard repudiating the new Scholasticism), others for it (St Ignatius inaugurating a new form of religious life suitable for new times). They have never ignored change. It is, nevertheless, a common reaction. When I was a young priest it was the prevalent reaction among British Catholics to new ideas about liturgy and ecumenism from the Continent. Led by our bishops, we turned our backs upon them and pretended that they did not exist.

The opposite temperamental response is also immature. This is to produce an instant judgement which owes little to thinking and a lot to feeling. It can, of course, take two forms: either back-to-the-wall conservatism or uncritical welcoming of everything new. We are familiar nowadays with both responses. There are some Christians for whom all change is simply unacceptable and wrong. They have made up their minds already about it, and no reasoning will change them. They persuade themselves that this response is virtuous and nail their colours to the mast of fidelity and loyalty. The flaw is that their reaction is instinctive, not reasoned, and therefore a matter of prejudice.

Sadly they do not help the genuine conservative cause. The opposite instinctive reaction is equally unhelpful. This is found in the person who embraces everything new just because it is new. Trendy followers of fashion are to be encountered in religion as much as anywhere else. We have experienced them in the Church since Vatican II. In the sixties they were enthusiastic secularists who loudly proclaimed they could not pray because for them God was dead, only to become enthusiastic members of prayer groups in the seventies in a similar unthinking way. Like the prejudiced conservatives these unreflecting followers of fashion do little to help the cause of genuine questioning and change. Dean Inge once said that the Church which marries the spirit of the age becomes a widow in the next generation. We should pause before we accept new religious fashions merely because they are new and are the fashion.

I do not wish to argue that all emotion is wrong and that we must be cold fish reacting only with our intellects to the world about us. That, too, would be profoundly inhuman. We are clearly right in being emotional about change. It shows that we care about the Church. But our judgements are meant to be reached by reason, accompanied but unclouded by emotion. We have the phrase 'make up our mind'. It is our mind which has to be made up when faced with modern issues, not our feelings. The mature person is the one who knows his temperament well enough to know the instinctive bias which he has, and takes that into account when making up his mind. The instinctive conservative will remember his temperament when faced with a novelty and ignore the signals of fear coming from deep down till he has made his judgement. The person with the tendency to trendiness will make himself pause before coming to conclusions and not be afraid to say no to an exciting new experiment if his mind tells him it is unwise. Faced with the problematic issues we have been discussing in this chapter the aim is to discover the truth. Our minds are there for that search. Our feelings are not. As in the game of bowls, we have to know the bias which is in us and then aim off accordingly. The player who forgets about the bias in his bowl ends up ludicrously far from the jack. The winner is the player who knows his bias so well that he uses it to get close to the target.

Prayer

For a Christian, discovering the truth is the same as discovering God's will. We believe that God has a will for the Church and for each of us singly. He is a Father, lovingly concerned about us, leaving us completely free but with a will for us every minute of the day. The Christian adventure is discovering that will and then having the joy of obeying it. Concerning these modern issues, then, our search is for nothing less than God's will in their respect. The armaments race, peace and justice, ecology, etc. – what does God want? That is our concern.

God is Lord of history, which is a way of saying that he respects man's freedom. He allows the course of history to run freely both when it is against and when it is for his purposes. Issues will arise and become acute at different times in mankind's history. It is man's task (under God who gives him freedom) to address himself to the issues and then seek their solution as they arise. This is bound to be bewildering to men living in the middle of it. This bewilderment is itself part of God's designs. It is the way he has made and makes the world. We should not, however, presume that the confusion we experience is in God. It is in us, part of the challenge thrown to us by God to know his will; but it is not in him. He knows clearly at all times what his will is. In other words, we have to accept the confusion of living at a time of cultural and religious change as part of living in history; but we must not lie down under it. We must not elevate bewilderment into an absolute and wallow in our muddles. The challenge is to campaign towards solutions of the various issues and never rest content till the right changes have been made and the wrong ones rejected. Incessant questioning is, as I have said, part of being alive. Finding answers to the questions is equally a sign of life. Not resting till answers have been found is in particular a sign of maturity.

Here we come up against a difficulty for the average Christian today. Simply put, the difficulty is that one is often incapable of finding a solution to the problems with which the world abounds. They are too big, too unknown for an ordinary busy person to come to a conclusion about them. One knows of them from newspapers but one does not have sufficient information to make a judgement. A moral problem in the local community can be solved by personal investigation, but how does one investigate, say, Britain's involvement in racialist regimes or the nation's penal system? Inevitably we turn to experts, both for information (technical experts) and for guidance (moral experts), and the first thing the experts often say is that there is no quick solution, that time is needed, that much research may have to be done. Meanwhile the ordinary Christian, who genuinely wants to do his Father's will, is left waiting. He is aware that to brush these problems under the carpet is wrong in spite of a strong temptation to do so. So what is he to do?

He must pray. While keeping before his mind the intellectual element in the problems, while facing the issues squarely and resisting the urge to run away and leave them to other people, while being content to be patient before these big problems, he must pray. He must pray because in prayer we are assimilated to the mind of Christ. It is not a quick process. I do not mean that we should pray for guidance and expect a solution to come at the end of the prayer. I mean that we should base our life on prayer, making it part of ourselves, so that after much practice and persistence we can hope to participate in the mind of God and so see things his way. Prayer unites us to God, and united with God we are given a share in his Spirit, which is the spirit of wisdom and knowledge. Filled with the Spirit we approach the problems of the modern world, as it were, from the other end, from the angle of God. St Paul described the process as that of acquiring the mind of Christ. We should, therefore, place ourselves firmly within the orbit of God, and become persons for whom prayer is the air we breathe, and God the most real Presence in our lives. This is quite different from saying prayers for guidance. It is the business of voluntarily opening our lives to the pervasive influence of God, his Holy Spirit. God's Spirit lives in all Christians. It is so easy to leave him there as a dormant element, instead of stirring those embers within us into flames. To enter into a life of prayer is to fan those flames into a fire of union with God.

We need have no fear that recourse to prayer will be an escape from the problems of our day. Prayer is no head-in-the-sand operation exonerating us from further effort to renew the Church and the world. True prayer has the opposite effect. It exposes us, without defences, to the will and purpose of God. As a result when a body of people gets down to prayer it releases spiritual forces in the group which up to then have been bound. A heartening feature in the Church in recent years has been the number of religious congregations which have met together to deliberate their future, often locked in conflict with each other and with seemingly no way forward. They have purposefully put themselves before God in prayer, and through that prayer have reached profound and progressive conclusions. Prayer has given them the mind of Christ and with it his guidance in their problems. In this, the religious congregations have followed the example of the bishops at the Vatican Council, who placed themselves in prayer before God when they began to deliberate their agenda. Could any of them in 1961 have foreseen their conclusions of 1964? The fact is that, while not shirking the intellectual spadework and debate needed, they opened themselves to the Holy Spirit and were carried forward to inspired conclusions.

True prayer is exposure to the purposes of God. So, when we engage in prayer we find that our instinctive defences against serious thought are melted away. Both the instinct to leave all the problems for others to solve and the instinct to rush into instant solutions look pretty silly when we pray. We realize that such reactions are essentially frivolous and do not stand exposure to the reality of God which prayer leads us to experience. It is *not* praying, rather than praying, that makes people irresponsible.

The Christian who prays involves himself in a double journey, a journey inwards and a journey outwards. The journey inwards is the journey from the issues of this world towards God. It is a journey towards the

17

mind of Christ, beyond feelings of expediency or fear of what people will say, to truth itself. It is followed by the journey outwards back from the depths where we meet God to the issues facing us in our everyday life, a journey which we now undertake with a new sensitivity to the will of God in all things. This double journey, or oscillation, takes place in us whenever we pray. It forms the rhythm of our life, a rhythm which is the rhythm of maturity. It is a two-way exposure. The journey inwards exposes us to God and the journey outwards pitches us back into God's world, and as with all pendulums the bigger the swing towards God in prayer the bigger the swing back towards the problems and persons of this world. It is a process that inevitably brings great pain and bewilderment, but it is a maturing process.

A chief gain from the inward journey of prayer is that it helps us in the task of distinguishing what is essential from what is accidental. In prayer we dip below the surface reactions of everyday life to a deeper area of living; we pass, to a certain extent, out of time into the timelessness of God. The experience of prayer helps us to separate what is passing and accidental from what is permanent and essential. We become less bothered about temporary forms (for instance, the language of the liturgy) and more concerned about God, who is approached through them. I do not claim that this discerning gift comes automatically to those who pray, but I think that those who possess it have been given it through opening themselves to God in prayer. In our parish there are certain ones who have a gift of disentangling what is essential from what is transient when faced with new things in the Church. Because they have a certain habitual disposition of living beneath the surface they remain content and smiling in the midst of all the storms that arise in the parish teacup. Incidentally they are not particularly intellectual people.

At a time of change this gift for discernment is precious. Christians are faced with a double loyalty which of its very nature brings tension. At times of change this tension is heightened. The tension is between being loyal to the gospel message which has been handed down through two thousand years of tradition as the word of God for us, and being loyal to the Spirit of God living in today's world, who speaks his word through contemporary voices in society. The sensitive Christian will be aware of both voices of God, each in its way calling for a loyal hearing and faithful following. In theory it is certain that God will not contradict himself, so there is no danger of a conflict of loyalties. In practice, harmonizing these two loyalties calls for honest work and much trust. Consider the issue of family life already mentioned. The spirit of the times (God's Spirit?) calls for quite a different relationship between wife and husband from what was prevalent a hundred years ago, and a different family attitude to children from that of the days when they were severely disciplined and expected to be seen and not heard. On the whole these changes seem to be inspired by God working through contemporary insights. But on the other hand, Christians are aware of the long tradition of discipline, respect and obedience combined with love which has existed down the centuries and which they believe they derive from the Holy Family at Nazareth. It is not always easy to combine loyalty to this tradition with a proper respect for the newer values of our age. It will only be done through prayer.

Knowing God's will for the average Christian is not

so much a learned pursuit in the field of ethics as a loving personal quest for God. In this way we are gradually assimilated to the mind of Christ and our knowledge of what to do becomes more instinctively certain and fixed on God. The opinion of experts continues to have its important place in our deliberations, but for living guidance we rely on communion with God in prayer. That communion makes us open to the demands of God and if, as so often happens, we have to wait all our lives for a definitive answer, then we recognize the hand of God in that too. For, sometimes, not even many years of prayer resolve the tensions or harmonize the contradictions, and we have to proceed in faith, neither abandoning the effort to understand nor jumping to hasty conclusions out of plain impatience. The demand for answers to our problems can stem from a self-sufficient hastiness which is far from God. God often leaves us in the humiliating position of not knowing what to do and being genuinely in two minds over an issue. As long as we remain open to him and continue searching, there is no harm and positive gain in this. It is, after all, his will, not our comfort which we seek.

Chapter Three

INTERIORITY

Reflection

Christians often go on retreat. They drop their everyday occupations and go somewhere quiet to reflect, before God, upon their lives. Retreat is not a very apt word for what they try to do since it suggests a running away from life, whereas the point of a retreat is precisely to face up to oneself and one's duties, and much of the time in a retreat is spent in investigating one's escape routes from duty and blocking them off. Nevertheless, the term remains valuable since it underlines the necessity of standing back from one's life from time to time in order to view and assess it better. Retreats are times for reflection, and reflection is a vital human act. It is part of being human and we cannot live our life at all without it.

I wonder if we think sufficiently about the joy of reflection. We human beings have this marvellous gift of being present in a situation bodily, while simultaneously being able to talk about it to ourselves, comment upon it, follow up any number of possibilities in our mind, as the situation unfolds itself. This reflection does not abstract us from things (it is not day-dreaming, which is thinking about things unconnected with the situation we are in), but on the contrary helps us to concentrate more intelligently upon what is going on. Reflection is our way, as human beings, of participating in events. We reflect on what may happen, has happened, could have happened, should have happened, will never now happen, and so on. To reflect as we converse is to bring a rich contribution to any gathering we are in. There are, as I said, times when we need to go away altogether from society in order to reflect in tranquillity, but the more important reflection we engage in is the reflection we bring to bear upon events while we participate in them. Reflection in retreat is useful as a specialized aid to the reflection which we should be doing all the time as we go about our daily life. Without the latter the former is mere waste of time.

One way of considering reflection is to notice that it is an interior occupation. When we reflect we turn in upon ourselves, go on a journey inwards. Outwardly we are still the same, but inside ourselves there is much activity as we think over what is happening and consider our reaction to it. The more we perfect ourselves in this the more profound we become. We uncover layers in our personality which are new to us. We begin to go deep into ourselves. The shallow person is the one who seldom reflects upon what is happening and so gives himself little opportunity to know his reactions. The 'interior' person is one who does reflect upon events, especially the ones he is involved in himself, and so gets to know his reactions and, with perseverance, himself.

I sometimes see reality as a giant water-lily covering the surface of a pond. There are innumerable flowers stretching over the water which on the surface are distinct from each other. But if you look beneath the water you see that the flowers are all connected and are merely the different blossoms of one huge stem.

What looks on the surface like a multitude of water-lilies is in fact one large one. For me, events in life are like those flowers on the surface of the pond. They appear to be distinct but in reality are inter-connected. Reflection is the art of looking beneath the surface to discern the interconnections. The novelist's injunction 'Only connect' is sound advice to anyone who wants to understand events.

It is not at first easy to see the interconnections in life. It is something which we hope will come with experience. Children do not see the connection between events and so everything that happens to them comes as a separate surprise, joyful or otherwise. Even adults take time to see connections. You have to reflect before you notice in history that the cultivated glories of the Greek city-states were only made possible by the institution of slavery. The democracy of those pioneer societies of free men needed slavery to make them work. The water-lilies of Plato, Aristotle, Demosthenes were connected beneath the beautiful surface with those other flowers, the slaves they owned. Similar unobserved connections exist in our own lives which only honest reflection can discover. As a priest who is in favour of progressive changes in his parish I have to remind myself that this is made possible by the large reserve of loyalty built up in the parish by unprogressive predecessors. There is a connection between my ability to make changes and my predecessors' unwillingness to do so. When I was a university chaplain I used to point out to students that their ability to be radical about society was made possible by the conservative history of the society they lived in. I hoped to show them that there is a certain element of luxury about being a left-wing member of a right-wing organization and that prior to exercising this luxury they should acknowledge the connection.

It is a mark of maturity to spot inconsistencies in one's behaviour or opinions. This kind of observation is an important part of making connections. I have listened at length to a businessman denouncing strikers in industry as unpatriotic. When it was pointed out to him that strikes were legal, he replied that, acting legally or not, strikers should put the good of the country before their own advantage. This businessman employed a chartered accountant to enable him to pay the least possible tax to the Inland Revenue. He explained that he was not breaking the law because his tax arrangements were perfectly legal. Furthermore it was common practice among his peers. He had not made any connection between his own putting self before country and that of the strikers he was condemning. Jesus' remark about spotting motes and being blind to beams was aimed at these sorts of inconsistencies in our lives. We need reflection to help us see such inconsistency.

Reflection also helps us to sort out the motivation of others and ourselves, and to detect the gap that sometimes exists between what is proclaimed openly to be one's motive and what deep down is the real motive. The difference between these two, my proclaimed motive and my real motive, is commonly acknowledged today. When the difference is conscious and deliberate, then I am being a hypocrite, saying one thing and meaning another. We do not need much self-knowledge to know when this is happening. When the gap between words and motivation is unconscious we encounter the 'rationalization' described by the psychologists. Rationalization occurs when the reason I give for doing something is not the real reason but one unconsciously produced so as to be acceptable. For instance, deep down I may be jealous of a colleague, so I exclude him from meeting people who mean a lot to me in case he wins them from me. I proceed to rationalize this exclusion to myself in any number of ways, thinking he should take a holiday, inventing jobs elsewhere for him to do, even engineering his removal, all the time convincing myself that I do it out of concern for him. I never actually admit that I am jealous. Clearly, by definition rationalization is unconscious, but we all need to be sufficiently reflective about our lives to know that we are prone to do it, and to know the occasions when this is most likely.

If we have experience of the rationalizing tendency in human beings we are in a position to help our neighbours when they come to us in trouble. So often the problem they first present is not the real problem but a simple, surface one. Our business is to be sympathetic and listen long enough until the real, deep-down problem emerges, the problem which is beneath the superficial, rationalized one first brought up. By knowing that this will happen, if we listen with sympathy we are able to be of help to our friends long after the surface problems they bring to us have been dealt with. The way we know that this will happen is not from books but by experience, especially the experience of ourselves in similar circumstances. Eckhart said, 'I know that if I knew myself truly I should know all creatures perfectly.' Honest reflection upon our own actions sets us on the way of knowing ourselves truly. This in turn should help us to know other people. It is once more a question of an inward journey (towards self-knowledge) being followed by a healthy outward journey to the world we live in. This is the rhythm of maturity.

Internalization of Values

The inward journey of knowledge leads to another inward journey in terms of our values. The more reflective we are in the face of circumstances the more we place our values and securities within ourselves in spiritual things, rather than outside ourselves in material goods. As we grow more reflective, get to know ourselves better from the inside, make more interconnections about ourselves and other people, we are impelled to produce a parallel 'internalization' of the values by which we live. We all have things we set our heart on, which determine our whole existence and 'make us tick'. For the miser it is money. For the aesthete it is beauty. For the average person it is a muddled assortment of things, ranging from the sublime to the ridiculous. The business of Christian growth is first of all to sort these values out according to the priorities, and then to internalize them, that is, to set out on the journey which begins with our hearts being fixed on a multitude of worldly goods outside ourselves and ends when we set our heart upon the deep interior good which Jesus once described as the One Thing Necessary.

There are various stages in this journey which mark the shift in interest from purely material possessions to more spiritual values. It would perhaps be better to say shift in securities, as interest is too weak a word. We are all from birth looking for security, looking to 'feel O.K.' in a more or less alien world. One of the ways in which we conquer these feelings of insecurity is by acquiring possessions. These make us feel O.K. We feel that if we become conspicuous owners we will be more secure and able to stand up among our fellow human beings. So we become men of property. Those behind the advertising industry know this well and play upon this sense of insecurity in us all. They persuade us that if we possess our own house, have a car of our own, smoke and drink plentifully, or, alternatively, wear a variety of clothes, use manufactured aids to beauty, have a lot of furniture, all will be well with us. There is a multiple appeal to our sense of property to possess much and so feel fulfilled. This appeal is, in addition, full of ramifications in our class-ordered society. We have to have the right sort of possessions, not just any sort, in order to feel secure, and the correct clothes, drinks, furniture in one class of society turn out to be incorrect for another! The right working-class furniture is hopelessly wrong for a middle-class home. Clothes for the teenage market will not do for the middle-aged. So the urge to possess is modified by the proviso that we have to possess the right things and not the wrong ones if we are to feel secure among our fellows. All this adds up to what for many can become the all-absorbing preoccupation of life. For most of us it certainly looms large in our concerns.

Jesus Christ had no time for this kind of living. He challenged his contemporaries to abandon these purely worldly and egocentric ambitions and seek first the Kingdom of Heaven. The first step in Christian conversion is to embrace poverty of spirit by simply dispelling those concerns about worldly possessions. For most of us this will not mean selling our possessions and leading a life of Franciscan poverty. It will, however, mean leaving behind a reliance on ownership of material things, for that was Christ's call to everyone. We are asked to recognize that material possessions do not constitute our security and that it lies elsewhere in the realm of the spirit. Jesus expects us to be quite ruthless in this first step of jettisoning our possessiveness and becoming poor in spirit. He indulged in no condemnation of material things as such. (They are good, created by God.) But he launched into a strict condemnation of rich people who set their heart on them and so did not have time or energy for spiritual things. The first growth point, then, in the Christian life is when we realize that material possessions are good things in themselves but must be spiritually surrendered in order that we may set our hearts on deeper things.

The first stage is to stop being possessive of worldly things. The second stage is to stop being possessive of spiritual things. The irony of human nature is that once we stop being selfishly preoccupied with our property, our furniture, our clothes, we can almost overnight become selfishly preoccupied with our spiritual possessions. The object of our possessiveness changes from food, drink, motorcars to prayer, virtue and the spiritual life; but the innate possessiveness itself does not change, and even sometimes grows. Have we not all seen that happen? Someone undergoes a spiritual conversion and is no longer materially orientated. He or she is now bound up with the things of the spirit: prayer, virtue, liturgy, the works of religion are now the chief preoccupations, and the material interests of the past are abandoned. But the old Adam is still there and, perhaps, thrives on his new spiritual diet. Egocentricity and personal ambition are still alive but are now engaged upon religious pursuits. The prayer group or the personal work of apostolate becomes the vehicle for pushing self forward. Spirituality becomes the new ego trip. I look back with shame to times in my life when I worshipped prayer (not God) and was internally arrogant about companions who in my opinion were not men of prayer. My conversion was only very superficial and consisted in a change of interests from worldly things to spiritual things but not yet a change of heart. Enthusiastic as I was for praying, I was on the whole as full of vanity as ever.

A Christian change of heart implies a deeper conversion than the superficial one of aims and interests. It implies a change deep down in our souls. We move from being possessive about either material or spiritual things towards not being possessive at all. This second change is truly Christian, because it means that Christ has turned us inside out. Our values change. What we set our heart on is no longer something that belongs to us (my spiritual life, my religious observances) but simply the Other, Jesus Christ and God his Father. We set our heart on God and surrender to him. His will becomes our chief pleasure. Because submitting to God's will is a surrender, not an achievement, our very possessiveness is destroyed at root. We learn to become poor in spirit. We learn to be filled with spiritual riches if God so wills, but also to be emptied of them when that also is God's will. (It sometimes is.) We become unconcerned about what happens in our souls, because we are concerned overwhelmingly with God. This implies a shift in values away from religious observances and spiritual experiences inwards to God himself dwelling in our souls. It is accompanied by more flexibility than before. We do not cling to something which we call our spiritual life. It ceases to matter much because God's presence now matters completely. The overwhelming concern is not to grasp spiritual riches, but to allow ourselves to be grasped by God. We learn to let go and let God take over. The turn-round is complete, from wanting to possess to wanting to be possessed, from an amassing of self-confidence

29

based on ownership to being stripped bare by God and left with only him to trust. Except in rare cases this does not happen overnight, but is a slow progress whose speed is dictated by God and not by ourselves.

Liberation

The chief fruit of this Christian change of heart is liberation. As long as we are dependent upon external things for our security and confidence we are not liberated. It matters little whether the dependencies which bind us are the material goods of the consumer society or spiritual good things like 'my work for the Church', 'my prayer group' or 'my religious life'. As long as we cling to them possessively, we are not free. Freedom only comes when our hearts are free. In other words freedom is an interior gift. It is the goal of the journey inwards. Of course it is connected with external freedom, but it is superficial, to say the least, to think that liberty is a question of being free only from external restraints. External restraints have little to do with real liberty or the lack of it. 'Stone walls do not a prison make nor iron bars a cage.' Human liberty is freedom of the heart, that is, it is freedom from internal restraints, from all those spiritual chains we forge for ourselves like jealousy, acquisitiveness, guilt, our uncontrolled fears and passions. Once these have been mastered, then indeed we are free, gloriously free to love God and men, and enjoy this world. But while we are still under the influence of an addiction, whether it be to the latest fashion or to a favourite form of prayer, then we are still in prison and in need of liberation. Our prison walls are erected by our unregenerate appetites which make us unable to say no to our native acquisitiveness for either worldly or spiritual advantage.

I am not advocating cultivating empty hearts which love nobody and nothing. That would be to advocate death. I am advocating life: not a dead heart with no love, but a changed heart, which has grasped the secret of Christian liberty. This is to love God absolutely (i.e. seek first the Kingdom of God) and then in the light of that absolute 'enslavement' to be sovereignly free with regard to all creatures, including oneself. To love no one is to be free, but with the vacuous freedom of death. To love God absolutely and to place total confidence in him and not possessions is to be supremely free, with the freedom and happiness of life. It is also to be inner-directed, dependent no longer on external circumstances for peace of mind and effectiveness, but conscious that the free union with God in the depths of one's heart is what one lives for and what 'makes one tick'. This is the liberation I spoke of, which is the terminus of the journey inwards. It is the supreme gift of the interior life.

John and Annie had been married over fifty years and in their old age I used to take them Communion at home. It was a joy to visit their home, because there was an uncanny spirit of peace in it. They sat together, watched a bit of television, and John, who was housebound, put a bet on the horses every day which Annie took down to the bookie at the corner. Then one day John had a cerebral stroke and died. Annie was left alone, utterly bereft. I tried to comfort her. She comforted me. 'Don't worry about me, Father, I'm at peace. John is with God.' Annie would not understand the term 'inner-directed', but when I use it I think of her. She lived for God, took everything that happened as part of his plan. She serenely enjoyed

31

life. Deep down she was united to God, so nothing could shake her. One of the things that struck me about John and Annie when they received Holy Communion in their house was that after receiving the Sacrament they both used silently to weep. They sat together, streaming with joy! For me it was a revelation of Jesus' idea about the One Thing Necessary. I used to tiptoe away, filled with awe.

Biblical Freedom

This development of spirituality in the Bible is a development towards interior freedom and love. The Old Testament Jews, being people of their day, had a very much externalized religion. The Law and the Temple were the twin pillars of their spirituality, both constantly in danger of being deified. Immense ritual slaughters of livestock took place in the Temple at Jerusalem, and the following of the prescriptions of the Law with external precision became increasingly the centre of Jewish spirituality. It was difficult to cultivate a religion of the heart in the face of such external ritualism. On the other hand there was a constant thread running through Jewish history of more interior, spiritual worship. The incident of the condemnation of the Golden Calf at the origin of their history reminded them that God could not be visibly portrayed and therefore the worship of God could not be contained by a purely external rite. When the Prophets came, they reiterated this theme and kept up a constant campaign against the Temple sacrifices, because they saw that the Jews could so easily substitute these ritual actions for the worship of the heart which God wanted. Amos, Hosea, Isaiah, Jeremiah, Joel can all be quoted against external ritualism and in favour of a religion of the heart in which morality and spiritual worship take first place. Joel's cry, 'Rend your hearts and not your garments', sums up this constant plea of the Prophets. God wants your heart in complete submission; the external ritual is only important if it helps that. There is a danger that you will think the external ritual is enough and use it as a substitute for the hard work of loving your neighbour and worshipping God. That sums up the message of the Prophets. They were not puritans who wanted no external ritual, but they were deeply spiritual men for whom the Temple rites were only valuable if there was an interior spirituality of love and mercy to accompany them.

The interior thrust of Jewish spirituality received new strength from the Prophets Jeremiah and Ezekiel at the time of the Exile. Jeremiah prophesied a new covenant between God and his people which would not be like the old covenant made at the time of Moses at the Exodus. This new covenant would be an interior one, written in the hearts of God's people. 'I will put my law within them, and I will write it upon their hearts; and I will be their God and they shall be my people' (Jer. 31:33). A few years later Ezekiel was saying a similar thing to the Jews in exile in Babylon. The future covenant at the time of the Messiah, he said, will involve a change of heart; it will be essentially an interior change. 'A new heart I will give you, and a new spirit I will put within you; and I will take out of your flesh the heart of stone and give you a heart of flesh' (Ezek. 36:26). In the course of history this message of the Prophets was obscured by the priests and scribes of official Jewish religion, but it seems to have been kept alive among the simple people of Israel when it was forgotten by their rulers.

Jesus came from those simple people. His message *was* that of those two sayings of Jeremiah and Ezekiel. For him, keeping the prescriptions of the Law was important, but more important still were the dispositions of the heart. The Sermon on the Mount takes the Ten Commandments and interiorizes them. Killing was wrong, but so was hating and resentment. Adultery was wrong, but so was lusting with the eyes. What, above all, was important was love. To treat God as Father and base one's life on that relationship rather than on observance of the Law was the essence of religion (Matt. ch.5). Through all the teaching of Jesus runs this message: that God the Father wants from us a pure heart, and the external actions of religion (for instance, prayer, fasting, almsgiving – Matt. ch. 6) are only valuable if they help or manifest this heart given to God.

It is not surprising that the spirituality of the early Church was a markedly interior one. Gone were the sacrifices and the Temple. In their place was the sacrifice of the heart (Rom. 12:1) and informal meetings for worship in private homes (Acts 2:42–47). Jesus' one all-sufficing sacrifice on the cross had abolished the necessity of further ritual sacrifices by men (Epistle to the Hebrews). Religious acts would still take place and be necessary, like prayer, prophecy, knowledge, faith that moves mountains, almsgiving and martyrdom, but they would all be valueless without love, the conversion of heart foretold by Ezekiel (1 Cor.13). The outstanding controversy of the early Church turned on this point of interiority. The convert Jews evidently found this new spiritual religion very naked and wanted to include the works of the old Law in the new Christianity. Having the Law to follow would give them religious security. They would know where they were, whether they kept it or broke it. St Paul took issue and fought for years to retain the simple religion of the heart which Christ had founded. Not the works of the Law nor any of those tangible things like almsgiving, prayer or prophecy constitute our salvation, was his teaching. It is simply faith in Christ (or love) which saves us. Trust God; do not trust in your works, was his message.

I find it moving to read St Paul and recognize that beneath his vigorous, exaggerated language he was fighting desperately to keep the interior heart in Christianity. His message was that we have been liberated by Jesus Christ, we are free. So let us not destroy this liberty by making new chains and prisons for ourselves, running back to the shelter of the Law, or any other external religious thing, in order to feel secure. Our security lies in pure faith, trust, love of God. Jesus will have lived and died in vain, he says, if we start placing our confidence in religious substitutes (presuming already that we have given up looking for material substitutes). In other words St Paul interpreted Jesus' teaching as a call for a totally inner-directed, liberated life of grace with God. It is a call to maturity, with childish dependencies put behind us and only trust in God left.

A girl once came to me whom I had known several years before. She had been living with her boy friend, had conceived a baby and then had had an abortion. Now she was overwhelmed with remorse. We talked it through at length and then I gave her sacramental absolution. She was mightily relieved but also a bit upset. Was it as easy as that? Could she go to Communion straightaway? Ought she not work her way back gradually and with penances? I explained to her that that would be trying to earn forgiveness. But she could not earn it. It was a free gift of God. She found it hard to accept forgiveness and salvation as a free gift. Most of us do. We want to win our way into heaven by our own efforts, like the Christian Jews who wanted the Law back in their religion in order to have a measurable target to achieve. It takes a lot of maturity to rely totally on Christ's grace and to have nothing tangible but only faith in God on which to base one's life. It takes a lot of maturity to be free.

Chapter Four

CONTEMPLATION

Maturity in Prayer

Like any other human activity prayer changes as it
matures in us. We grow into it just as we grow into
other activities like cooking or playing a musical
instrument. It is difficult to describe prayer because it
is the most deeply personal of our activities and
therefore likely to be different for each person. Also,
it is concerned with God, and that element makes all
description inevitably fall short of the reality. I will,
nevertheless, try to describe the growth in prayer which
takes place when Christians yield to the Holy Spirit
and set about praying seriously. At least in general
terms there seems to be a pattern which all follow as
they progress spiritually. I describe seven happenings,
but they are not steps in a sequence. There is no order
in which they take place, because in fact they are
simply seven descriptions of one growth and all seven
happenings take place simultaneously.

*The mind in prayer ceases to follow a process of reason-
ing.* Narrative, discourse, argument fade away in favour
of an intuitive dwelling upon the reality of God. The
mind stands still, not dead but more alive than ever
with wonder and joy. It is as if standing in front of
a painting we stop analysing its structure and form, its
colour, its points of artistic technique, and begin to

37

look at it and enjoy it as a whole, as the painting it is. So, in prayer, we find ourselves no longer talking to ourselves point by point about God's revelation and its meaning for us, but simply opening our hearts to him in one plain intuition of his presence. It is a marvellous breakthrough.

In prayer words diminish and sometimes stop altogether. Their place is taken by a silence which, at the risk of using an over-worked cliché, I would describe as meaningful. In other words not an empty, tedious silence, but a silence charged with 'communication' and vital love. The honest attempt to say what is in our hearts by piling words upon each other gives way to the realization that all words fail before the exciting and sublime reality of God and that silence is better communication. It comes as a relief to discover that we can be still and silent with God and that this mysteriously 'says more' than all our previous words. This happens in deep friendships and between lovers. Great passion is best conveyed in speechlessness. 'Words fail me' is a genuine experience in prayer and is a sign of growth if it happens naturally and is not forced. Just as there is no greater contentment than in the silent communion between two people who understand and love each other, so in personal prayer between ourselves and God we find ourselves resting contentedly in God's presence, our hearts stilled to silence, aware only of him and ourselves. It happens in prayer groups as well as to the individual. When a group has prayed together for some time it falls naturally into a communal silence which it finds relaxing, charged with the presence of Jesus Christ.

Thinking diminishes and loving grows. It is not that our minds become empty in prayer, but too full! Outside prayer it is perfectly possible to think rationally about God, but inside prayer we find our thinking faculty seizing up when faced with the immense reality of God. Simultaneously our heart brims over with love. In other words our mind holds on to one thought, the thought of God, and stays with it in a daze while the heart expands in love. The mind is not empty but replete with God, and because God is so far beyond human grasping the effect is of being dazzled with darkness rather than illumined with light. It is like when we look directly at the sun and see blackness instead of light. In this happy 'darkness' our prayer comes to rest.

Activity in prayer diminishes, passivity grows. The deeper we go in prayer the more it is given to us to see that we are passive in the Spirit's hands, that what is wanted of us is not activity to grasp God but pure receptivity as we let God grasp us. At the outset of prayer we set out to achieve a relationship with God, approach him with prayer-acts like thanksgiving, contrition, praise – in a word, we try to grasp and master God. This can become quite frenzied at times. Then reality breaks through and we know that we must be passive, like clay in the potter's hands. 'Thou mastering me, God' becomes our prayer, and in the wordless intuition of love we rest passive in the arms of God. It usually takes some time for us to learn to be passive towards God. Once learnt, huge relief and relaxation in the fact of God's Fatherhood become the central experience of our faith. This is not the same as a quiet life, because passivity to the Spirit of God means that we are more than ever before at the disposal of God's will; consequently a life of busy activity in God's service is likely to follow. The lives of saints and mystics bear witness to that. They show us that spiritual quiet is not so much an activity in itself which we engage in, doing nothing else, but a disposition of the heart which accompanies us in our busy activity for the Kingdom of God. Passivity with regard to God is not a thing we do but a way we have of doing things for him. Prayerful people are often busy people, but they have a serenity about them which is part of their effectiveness. It comes from their habit of waiting on God inside themselves.

Intellectual clarity diminishes, bafflement increases. The closer we get to God the more we see that human words and argument do not grasp his reality at all. In theory anyone who studies the science of God knows about this infinite gap between what our human words about God convey and the divine Reality itself. The fruit of contemplative prayer is to understand this not only notionally but really. As we kneel in prayer the oft-quoted phrase 'cloud of unknowing' becomes an experienced reality where before it was an intellectual concept. This growth in ineffability is an additional reason why silence instead of words becomes acceptable in prayer. We find it more real to express our bafflement before God in silence or short words like 'God', 'Love', 'Sin'. Lengthy argument or wordy praying just does not help. It gets in the way and seems rather hollow.

Consciousness of self diminishes, consciousness of God grows. Prayer begins with reflection, making those connections between the events of life and God which I spoke about in the previous chapter. Inevitably this increases self-consciousness. It heightens our awareness of ourselves. At this stage prayer is little more than talking to oneself about God and life. The breakthrough comes when we realize that God is personal – a person out there loving me, not just an idea in my mind. All at once prayer becomes a friendship, an I-thou relationship. It involves us in the Other. By implication,

40

as with all relationships, it takes us out of ourselves. This is the beginning of a process by which everything to do with our side of the prayer relationship fades in importance because it is overshadowed by the immense reality of God. All our religious acts like praise, thanksgiving, sorrow first of all coalesce into one religious act which can be described as surrender or abandonment to God. (St Paul's 'spiritual sacrifice' in Rom. 12:1). Our prayer becomes totally occupied with surrender to God. The next stage in growth is when consciousness of this surrender fades away and prayer becomes simply the reality of God! God looms so large that we forget about what we are supposed to be doing, about our 'spirituality'. It is God alone who matters. He fills the whole room and we are engulfed in him. We stay there because God stays there. He is the whole of reality now.

I have tried to describe in six ways what happens when prayer develops in a Christian. To recapitulate those six happenings may help us to see what a rich growth there is. One's relationship to God becomes intuitive; silent; loving; passive in the hands of God; ineffable; overwhelmed with the sheer presence of God. A seventh description does no more than reinforce what has already been said. *Prayer descends beneath the surface of life and enters into the depths of our personality.* As long as it is active, conceptual and full of words, prayer takes place at the surface of our being. Those sorts of activities are surface ones and to a certain extent outward-going. At that stage prayer is a journey outside ourselves terminating in an achieved relationship with God which is capable of being described in words. Growth comes with the death of all that activity and thinking. The grain of wheat, which is our initial approach to God, dies, and we are left with that other approach which is not an approach at all but a being approached by God. Prayer ceases to be an active journey outwards and becomes a journey into the depths, involving a succession of 'openings' to God, each one at a deeper level than the one before. It terminates excitingly at union with God himself, dwelling in the depths of our being, who has all along been waiting for us there.

The Journey Inwards

One way of praying is to go on a journey inwards. Begin by sitting upright with a straight spine. It is no good sprawling or slumping as we are sometimes tempted to do. You must wait for God with an upright relaxed attitude of the whole being. Then place your mind inside your body, making it stay in the body here and now. Contrary to popular opinion it is not the body which is the chief source of distraction in prayer, but the mind. The body stays where it is put, will stay obediently in a chair, in a church, until it is told to move. Not so the mind. It is by nature restive and questing, and does not remain with the body for long. It flies out of the window like a bird, visiting places in imagination sometimes miles away from where one is. It also goes on journeys in time, flying backwards in memory and forwards in anticipation – anything rather than remain in the present. To anchor the mind down in the here and now and still its wanderings it is necessary to keep it within the body which is always here and now. This is a worthwhile discipline, surprisingly hard (try it and see), but indispensable for prayer. Until one has got one's mind settled into the here and now it is not worth going further in prayer.

God is met in the concrete here and now, not an imaginary elsewhere.

Three things follow in sequence. You let go of all plans and worries and release them completely into the hands of God. When your prayer is over you will take back your responsibility for them, but just now you let them go into God's hands. You know that they will be looked after by him. It sometimes requires a big act of trust to do this and stop worrying, especially when there is a serious worry on your mind. It is an act of trust which brings great rewards. Then you settle, and wait on God, passive and expectant, trying to remain perfectly still in an attitude of waiting, patient, open, expectant, making a deliberate effort to 'slow down'. After a while you are ready to move into a third state which is to let God carry you. God comes to you who have disposed yourself to wait for him. He picks you up and carries you. You are close to him and completely dependent on him. You remain that way with him.

Now you begin the journey inwards, travelling down inside yourself to that still point in the centre of your being where you are most simply yourself. We all have this still centre, but we do not often visit it consciously. We are so often journeying in the other direction, going outwards to people and our daily tasks, that we take for granted this absolute centre inside ourselves. It is a worthwhile act to stop for a moment and think downwards into this centre, because it is the source of our identity as persons. 'Who am I?' can only be answered by travelling down inside ourselves. To let our identity come from our social and business activities exclusively is to run the risk of having twenty different personalities, which means in the end having no personality. In the final analysis my personality depends on who I am in myself, apart from my reactions to other people. It depends on what is going on inside me in the deep centre. The exciting Christian truth is that our deep centre is not empty. It is occupied by God, who dwells in all men. From Revelation we learn that God's dynamic, creating, loving Energy, which we call the Holy Spirit, lives and acts in the heart of all our beings. The journey inwards, then, to our deep centre is a journey towards God, who is already there waiting for us. We are travelling towards conscious union with him when we go on this inward journey. Some find it helpful to repeat a succession of phrases to help penetrate downwards to this still centre. *God within* : *God here* : *God now* : *God is* : *God*. Said slowly in succession these phrases act as signposts for the spiritual journey. The prolonged silence between the saying of each phrase is, of course, what constitutes prayer.

When we penetrate to the still centre and find God there, we simply let go into God, accept that he is the ground of our being, sink and merge into him. This sinking and merging is our conscious activating of the union with God which we have enjoyed as a gift since baptism. This baptismal union with God is there all the time. The Holy Spirit is in us. We are in Christ. God is deep down our Father. This is true at all times, unless we deliberately repudiate it by grave sin. In prayer, however, we consciously activate this union, make it live, deliberately think it through and surrender to God in the depths of our person. Sometimes we experience a melting and coalescing which assures us of the union. At those times it is inexpressibly vivid and experienced as 'real'. We can find no appropriate words to describe it. At other times there is nothing particular except a dryness, but the union is going on then too. A helpful succession of signpost phrases at this point is: *Ground of being : Let go : Sink and merge : Union.* The slow repetition of these words with plenty of silence in between can make the union heavy with significance. It is important to associate the body with what is happening in prayer. This can be done by making ourselves aware of our breathing and slowing it down. Breathe in – pause – breathe out – pause. Taking this slowly the body can be associated with the union which is being activated in our soul. Setting up this rhythm can help to tranquillize our being, and so deepen and prolong the union in our centre. Body and soul together enjoy union with God in deep peace and seriousness.

The final act of this prayer is to take up our responsibilities which we have let go into the hands of God. We place our hands once more upon the plough (but now conscious of God's hand powerfully covering our own). We open our eyes to meet the God we have been interiorly contacting, present in other people and in the world which is his creation. This we do slowly and prayerfully as a prelude to our Christian action, which is resumed with a lighter heart as a result of the seriousness of our prayer.*

Walking with God

I have described the journey inwards when it is done at set times of prayer. At these times one is usually in church or in some private place on one's own. The

---

* A schematic presentation of this way of praying can be found in the Appendix at the end of this book.

good thing, however, about this relationship of prayer is that it can be exercised at all times and in all places. Just because it is a journey inwards and not dependent on any exterior 'apparatus' like a church, or hymns and books, it can be done anywhere where we are kept waiting for a few minutes. At a bus stop, or queueing in a shop, or boiling a kettle, we find ourselves entering upon the journey inwards, allowing our deepest self to fuse with God, to sink and merge into the reality of the Trinity, as we simply wait. Nothing changes exteriorly, but inside is all fervour. We have phrases in English about the heart: 'lost my heart to', 'broken heart', 'put new heart into'. Each of these phrases corresponds with an experience of union with God in our daily activity. As grace takes over, we have a strong conviction that we have lost our hearts, that now more than ever they belong to Another and that we may no longer claim rule over them, since it is God who dwells and rules there. At times also we feel that something inside us has been broken. The fracture is not injurious to ourselves – on the contrary it seems to be fruitful and almost a healing fracture. It appears to be a wound that is going to be permanent, but a wound which will remind us constantly of our divine Lover to whom our hearts now belong and who energizes our every action. It is by no means a handicap to have had one's heart broken by love of God. Finally we undergo the experience of having new heart put into us. As we go about our daily, sometimes humdrum work we feel in our inner centre that there is new strength and new hope in what we do, because Jesus Christ is King of all the earth and we are enlisted by his love to spread his kingdom. The journey inwards has given us new heart for the many outward journeys we undertake in life. That is why, incidentally, the habit of praying at bus stops and in shop queues does not cut us off from our fellow human beings, as might be expected, but, paradoxically, makes us more aware of them and attentive to their needs.

The problem faced by all who have this experience of union with God is that the rest of one's life is seemingly unaffected by this tremendous inner drama. Inside one experiences being given wholly to God, surrendered and not belonging to oneself, but the rest of one's life seems out of step with the experience. It is almost as if there are two persons, the inner and the outer. It is puzzling to know which is the real one. I remain full of selfishness and sin, sometimes crippled with inhibitions and fears, flooded with unworthy thoughts, suspicions, aggressiveness, sensuous desires, on the whole mediocre and not very effective. The humiliating thing is that I am trying not to be these things but failing in my efforts. This I know is the real me. But that other me who experiences fusion with God in the centre is also real. I cannot deny what is happening deep down. (Though I get attacks of misgivings when I suspect it is all psychological delusion and doubt whether God exists. These are bad moments, which in the short term I answer with naked acts of faith and in the long term with a serious review of my situation as honestly as possible.) Meanwhile the course ahead seems to be to live through this tension between my outer and inner selves in as trusting a manner as possible, looking forward all the time, not back.

Two things can be said about this contradictory experience: first, that it is surely an interim position. Unless I give in to sin and fall back (an ever-present possibility) the hope is that God will lead me forward in his own good time and eradicate the selfishness and sin from my life, infuse courage into me to overcome my cowardice, purify me and my life so that I measure up to the standards set by Christ for all who receive the Spirit. It is my hope that this will happen. I know that it will not be done without suffering. In other words, God has taken over the centre of my being and wants to move outwards and take over my life and activities too. It is up to me not to resist the rising tide from the centre.

The second observation is the important one that this is the meaning of grace. God gives with sovereign freedom. He chooses the weak to confound the strong. There is no question of merit. It just happens that he unites himself with sinners while they are still sinners, disregarding their mediocrity and ungodliness. He chooses to love whom he chooses to love. It is a complete mystery. The lesson all Christians have to learn is that union with God is not a reward for past services but a gift (at baptism) for sinners, a gift which is followed by more and more gifts which also are not rewards for merit, but continue to be unearned surprises. In other words God is a lover who delights in showering graces upon the most unlikely and undeserving of us his children. We are not in a well-ordered meritocracy but a family with a rather crazy, loving Father. It is humiliating for the children who have been granted these graces to know that they are undeserved. The only danger, however would be if they began to think otherwise.

The reader will notice that I have been talking exclusively about personal prayer, describing the union between one soul and God in private. Many people today feel uneasy about this and want more stress placed on group prayer and liturgical community prayer. Clearly liturgical and group prayer are important, but I have chosen to stress individual prayer precisely because of the danger that personal prayer may be lost in the present climate in which group praying is stressed so much. I am in favour of emphasizing the need for community. Anyone who works in a city knows of the desperate loneliness which individuals in the crowd experience and of the need at all levels for more community living. I know how difficult it is for some to make relationships and how they can cut themselves off in miserable isolation because of a defect in their upbringing, sometimes directly stemming from their past Christian education. I am happy, therefore, about the growth of prayer groups in parish life. But I also sense dangers. The chief danger is that people who should be facing up to themselves and God in private as well as embarking upon community experiences may be tempted to bypass the solitary experience. If a person has never faced up to himself, is scared of being alone, feels only half a person unless in a group, then he (or she) may be running away by joining a prayer group. Such a person ought to face himself as an individual on his own as well as taking refuge in a group. Who am I when there is no one else in the room? is a question we must all ask ourselves. If the answer is that I am only partly living when solitary and get my identity from reacting and belonging to other people, then I ought seriously to face this problem and try to solve it by first of all meeting myself and then meeting God. Meeting God alone is an experience which we ought not to postpone. When we die we will meet God by ourselves. When attending deathbeds I am often struck by how alone the dying person is. The entire family is round the bed. I am there holding the person's hand, praying and supporting – but the dying man seems to be alone, facing his God, naked, defenceless. He is now beyond our support. If you and

I have consistently run away from the awesome experience of meeting God alone in prayer, we will be quite unprepared when it comes irrevocably at death. It seems to me that we should not be too ready to join with others for prayer unless we also face the experience of praying seriously by ourselves.

To join a community in any activity without first trying to solve one's personal problems honestly means that one may project those problems on to the group, and even end up by persuading oneself that they are the group's problems, not one's own. Sometimes conducting a retreat in a community I have met (the first night) a candid member who explains all the shortcomings of the community in detailed clarity. It does not take long to spot that this community member is really detailing his or her failings and to guess that the community has a problem on its hands in bearing with this member. Those who 'go on about' community are nearly always those who find it difficult to be members of a community. If we are tempted to go on about group prayer we should perhaps look into our personal life first before taking refuge in the group.

Some experiences of being alone are frightening. One which is merely irritating is being kept waiting. Modern life is full of that. We wait in queues almost everywhere; in traffic drivers and pedestrians are constantly kept waiting; telephone operators tell us to hang on and leave us in mid-air; people come late for appointments. These unavoidable moments can be turned into important moments by the journey inwards. Someone keeps us waiting; there is nothing we can do but wait; it would be wrong to go off and do something else. So instead of pacing up and down like a caged animal, we can go on the journey inwards. We can turn inwards, sitting or standing perfectly still, penetrating to the inner still point and merging into union with God who dwells there. If the waiting goes on for ten or fifteen minutes, thank God for this precious space, an unlooked-for interlude when the day began. On other occasions we may have only just begun to pray when the person comes. In both cases, this interlude of prayer makes us more serene and, in fact, more prepared for whatever is about to take place. De Caussade's phrase 'the sacrament of the present moment' describes this well. We seize the opportunity of the present moment and turn it into a meeting with God. A moment used thus brings grace to our souls. The joy of it is that we need no external apparatus for this kind of praying. What structure there is is entirely internal; no scaffolding is required. This means that we can, if we like, pray all the time and everywhere and will become eventually independent of circumstances. To this development we are called at baptism, not to a state of despising external religion but to a state of liberation from servitude to it. The fully grown Christian is the one who can reach out to touch God in any circumstances and does not demand a specially prepared approach without which he cannot pray.

Chapter Five

OUTER AND INNER

The Religious Ladder

When Jacob, on his way to find a wife among his kinsfolk, had his dream at Bethel, he saw 'a ladder set up on the earth, and the top of it reached to heaven; and behold, the angels of God were ascending and descending on it. And behold the Lord stood above it' (Gen. 28:12). Years later when Jesus recruited the sceptical Nathanael into his band of followers he promised that Nathanael would see 'heaven opened, and the angels of God ascending and descending upon the Son of man' (John 1:51). The image of a ladder set up between God and mankind, coming from the middle of the earth and reaching into the heart of God, pitched, in fact, 'between Heaven and Charing Cross', is a good one for religion. Religion is the man-made apparatus which we erect as a vehicle for the coming and going, the 'commerce', of our faith. Faith and love are intangible, spiritual activities which are beautifully evoked by the picture of those angels going up and down between us and God. Religion, on the contrary, is the visible, tangible, cultural apparatus of our spirituality. It is the outward sign of our faith. It is the ladder upon which the angels move.

Religion has three main aspects. First there is the aspect of belief, the whole intellectual system which we fabricate in our approach to God, as we try to understand our faith. It is expressed in creeds, catechisms, teaching formulas. Men have to know what they subscribe to as followers of a religion, so all religions have creeds which express their doctrines. In Christianity the Apostles' Creed is the basic formula to which all give assent. Next there is the aspect of code. This is the collection of moral precepts by which a religion orders its ethical life. Religions are ways of life, not just academic ideas, so they consider their moral codes important. By these they regulate the conduct which is acceptable and unacceptable for their followers. As Christians we are bound not only to believe in the Creed but also to follow the New Testament way of life taught by Jesus and embodied in passages like the Sermon on the Mount and his Two Commandments of love. After creed and code comes cult. Worship is important in all religions. It is what distinguishes them from ethical societies. It might almost be said that religion exists to give worship to God. You cannot have a religion which does not offer worship to the deity, in some form or other. Religion, then, is an interconnected amalgam of creed, code and cult. They are the three aspects of that ladder between us and God, the three connected ways in which our faith, trust and love of God find expression.

I remember a wartime Fougasse cartoon which consisted of two coloured pictures. The first was of a collection of men and women in khaki, at the outbreak of war, a mixture of ranks and regiments, all dressed in the one dull wartime colour. The second picture was of the same group of people in the same uniforms a few years after the war had begun. Now their khaki was enlivened everywhere with additions of colour: brown, green, purple, red had appeared in the caps and berets; red, white and blue in the lapel tabs; flashes and badges of all colours in the rainbow were being worn on the khaki uniforms. I do not remember any words under the pictures. The message got home without any words. Mankind is incurably differentiating. Put them all in the same uniform, and before long they will have diversified themselves into fifty different coloured variations of the original, simple khaki. What struck me most when I saw it was how exactly true it was of our wartime armed forces.

How true it also is of religion! As a religion develops and spreads among men it inevitably becomes diversified. The original simple idea of the founder becomes complicated as it is embraced by new peoples, attacked and defended in the course of time. The idea remains but is now more complex, the complexity having arisen from its development in situations which were not present when the religion first began. In Christianity the teaching of Jesus concerning truth and life progressed hugely from the simple, stark sayings of the Gospels. The sayings about truth were enshrined in ever more complicated creeds, then formal doctrinal statements of Church councils, then the writings of theologians. The sayings about life became codified through the ages into complex manuals of moral precepts. There is nothing sinister about this. It is a healthy sign that succeeding generations have taken the gospel message seriously and used it to guide their way through their own problems of life. The uniform of Christianity which we all receive gets modified and enriched as we wear it in differing situations through history.

This law of increasing complexity is especially true about the worship area of religion. Human beings differ so much, as do the circumstances they find themselves in, that it is not surprising that the ways in which they worship also differ greatly. Creed and code are less individual than cult, which is after all a deeply personal response, special for each generation and each individual. Hence that aspect of the religious ladder called worship and spirituality is bound to be the most diversified of all. The ways in which we approach God and express our faith are many and varied. Not only do different persons express their worship differently, but also one man in the course of his life will develop considerably in the way he communes with God and pray differently at the age of fifty from the way he did when twenty. The ladder of religion begins to appear rather complicated as more people use it to express their simple faith and 'ascend and descend' between heaven and earth.

A further point needs to be noticed about religion. Since it is the incarnational element in our response to God, it is by definition almost completely determined by human culture. The culture which moulds me will mould my religion. If it does not, is in some way prevented from moulding my religion, then my religion is not fully mine and there is an awkward gap between how I normally express myself and how I am expected to express myself religiously. When religion is most genuine it adopts the culture of its adherents and fits like a well-tailored suit. In other words Japanese Catholics ought to worship God in quite a different way from, say, Mexican Catholics or Scottish Catholics, if their religion is genuine. I once attended Mass said by an Indonesian cardinal. He sat throughout cross-legged on the ground before a low coffee-table 'altar'; the offertory procession was a beautiful dance by some girls who brought up flowers and strewed them on the floor all round the altar; the language and music were Asian. It was the Mass all right, but culturally foreign to a European, a distinctly different ladder from the one I am used to going up and down in my religious life.

It hardly needs saying that although religious cultures differ all over the world and through history, Christian faith, hope and love remain the same. There is a difference between the two. Faith, the inner spirit of response to God, is one thing. Religion, the outward expression determined by a people's culture, is another. At this point let us merely note the difference and, in particular, note the obstacle to a deepening of real spirituality which can be caused by failing to observe the difference. In the years after the Council of Trent the Catholic Church made a remarkably successful attempt to link its inner spirit to one form of outward expression. The inner kernel of Christian spirituality, our total abandonment to God in Christ, was tied all over the world to a particular European style of religious expression. Few people noticed the oddity of this at the time. Many readers, like myself, must have assumed this to be the divinely ordained scheme of things. The outstanding example is the Mass, which was said in Latin in every corner of the world regardless of the native culture. But there were many other assumptions that Counter-Reformation culture was the only permissible 'ladder' for Catholics all over the world – for instance Roman theology, Italian devotions, Spanish mysticism. They were all exported without alteration outside Europe to mission countries. Although an impressive uniformity was achieved, none of these forms of religion really suited non-European peoples, with the result that there was a block in the flow of the Spirit in many new converts. In Africa I have attended Mass in Latin with Gregorian chant in one traditional diocese and then a few days later moved to a post-Vatican-II-minded diocese where Mass was celebrated in the local language with vernacular songs and exuberant participation: the Spirit seemed to be chained in the former liturgy and marvellously released in the latter. There was no doubt in my mind which ladder was better suited for the upward and downward passage of Christian love.

Religion and Faith

The connection between religion and faith is a delicate and intimate one. In describing it one has to be careful not to fall into either of two mistakes. The first mistake is the one already mentioned of being so impressed by the union between the two that one virtually identifies them as one and the same. The danger of this is that one fails to distinguish between what is absolute and what is relative in Christian spirituality and treats the absolute and the relative with equal devotion and tenacity. The sacred loyalty due to Christ and his Church is given to the various interim cultural forms Christ's Church has taken in history. Cultural form is identified with the essence of Christianity itself. This is, in the final analysis, lazy thinking. If someone says he would die for the Mass he is expressing ideal Catholic sentiments. If he says he would die for the Latin Mass he is falling into the error of identifying a passing form with permanent substance. It is true that at any given moment a religious clothing for faith is absolutely necessary; but that is not the same as saying that any particular form of religious clothing is absolute. The necessity of having a religious expression for our faith is by no means the necessity of having one particular expression. There could never be any developments and changes if this were so. Imagine attributing to things like Gregorian chant, guitar folk music, the rosary, the clerical collar, priestly celibacy the same essential 'over my dead body' absoluteness which we attribute to the divinity of Jesus, the primacy of Peter, the Mass, the pre-eminent place of Mary among the saints. We must avoid confusing relative things with absolute things and so becoming intransigent over the former when all that is needed is to defend the latter.

The second mistake over religion and faith is one which in adopting the overall viewpoint of this book we run the risk of embracing. This is to make so much of the distinction between the two that one produces a two-tier spirituality with an upper tier of not very significant external actions and a lower tier of disembodied, deeply significant faith. This is to over-spiritualize religion. It is a process which ends up by disregarding the external material aspect and even despising it in favour of a purely interior religion of the spirit. Spiritually minded people face this as a constant temptation. It is tempting for them to look upon material actions like eating and drinking, dancing and singing, painting and sculpting as having nothing to do with religion. Like Savonarola or John Knox they denounce these as works of the flesh. In doing so they divide man into two beings, body and soul, two separate spheres of interest; and they place the realm of religion firmly in the sphere of the soul and exclude the body from it. This is simply wrong, because man is not two beings, but one. He is an embodied soul, one person, who cannot perform purely bodily actions in which his soul does not take part nor purely spiritual actions where the body has no place. When man acts he acts as one person, producing one spiritually embodied act whether it is eating and drinking or thinking and praying. Body and soul together do both.

There is only one tier in spirituality, that of the whole person, in which the 'body' is given as much importance and reverence as the 'soul', because these are merely aspects of the human being, shorthand designations for the direction in which the person is acting. So in Christian spirituality eating and drinking, dancing and singing, painting and sculpting all have their honoured part to play. The Christian sacraments are precisely that: ritual actions in which the outer material thing done (e.g. eating) itself embodies the inner spiritual thing received (e.g. the grace of Holy Communion), and material things are neither despised nor bypassed. So in our talk about religion and faith we must not fall into thinking that religion, the man-made apparatus, does not matter and that only faith, the inner devotional core, does. What matters is to see that religion is always an appropriate embodiment for faith, and the work of doing this involves us in distinguishing between what is essential and what is not. Like the snake which keeps alive by sloughing off its old skin and letting a new one grow, so our faith has to adopt new religious forms in order to preserve its inner fire and devotion. In that sense, making a distinction between devotional forms (religion) and inner commitment (faith) is important.

The process of getting rid of old skin and acquiring new skin takes time. First comes a period of destruction. This is followed by a vacuum in which nothing lives. This in turn is followed by a fertile period of the birth of new forms. It is the Good Friday, Holy Saturday, Easter Sunday sequence. In the last ten years Catholic devotional life has passed through this passover process.

Destruction came first. The much loved traditional devotions suddenly began to lose their following – Benediction, Quarant' Ore, the Novena, Rosary devotions, Stations of the Cross. Most people seemed no longer interested in these exercises which used to fill the churches. Anxious priests met together to study why the fall-off had occurred. It seemed to be universal. Many explanations were found. Clearly it had much to do with the Vatican Council, but whether the Council was cause or effect was not clear. Among many priests Pope John came in for blame, which was all the more baffling when his spiritual journal was published and it was seen what a thoroughly 'devotional' Italian Catholic he had been. For those who loved the Devotions it was 'Good Friday' indeed. There followed the vacuum of 'Holy Saturday' during which the devotional side of Catholic life seemed virtually dead. There was talk of an age of Religionless Christianity beginning, even that God was dead. During this period I was a university chaplain. Students showed themselves uninterested in all spiritual devotions other than the Mass (with the curious exception of all-night vigils). Politics, rather than religion, became the popular and vital expression of faith. It was a spiritually purgative, desert-like, era. Nothing devotional lived.

I am now back in parish work and am participating in the 'Easter Sunday' of religious devotions. New forms are springing up everywhere. It is difficult to keep up with them. It is a period of great fecundity. The desert has flowered. Bible-study groups, discussion groups, prayer groups, charismatic or otherwise, Focolare groups, the Movement for a Better World: we have all these in the parish. There may well be more to come. So far from being religionless, our faith seems to be fuller than ever of religious forms. They are not, of course, the old religious forms, but they seem to have as much drawing power as the old ones, though they operate in significantly different ways (small house-based groups rather than large church-filling assemblies). The partnership between religion and faith seems to be as productive as ever. Outer and inner are coming together again after the uneasy period of transition from old to new.

The Grammar of Spirituality

True contemplative prayer does not lead us away from outward religious forms, but it does lead us to deepen our attitude towards them. We continue to use that ladder pitched between us and heaven, but the way in which we use it changes. I can best describe this by saying that it ceases to be a noun for us and becomes an adverb. When we are first introduced to religion and begin to use its spiritual practices these practices themselves loom large in our mind. The routine of morning and night prayer, the rosary, the divine office, or other spiritual plans occupy the centre of our attention. We fix our purpose upon them and commit ourselves to them. This is true of all beginnings, both the beginnings of religion as a child, and that second beginning which a novice in a religious order makes, or someone who has been spiritually reawakened in, say, a prayer group. In all these cases the new practice is loved for its own sake and becomes the object of commitment. We have all met the novice who is striving with all his powers to love the Rule by which he lives, and the Legion of Mary girl who 'loves the Legion'. These are people who have found a new centre for their lives and are passionately devoted to it. This is what I would call treating the ladder of religion as a noun.

In God's good time commitment to a form of religion leads to a subtle change. Almost imperceptibly the Christian's love and attention is drawn away from religious forms to God himself. It would be better to say it is drawn *through*, rather than away, because what happens is that the love and commitment to religious practices goes on but is drawn through them to the Object they all point to, viz. God. In other words the religious practices become adverbs rather than nouns in our grammar of religion. Thus I continue to participate in the liturgy, but instead of loving the liturgy it would be truer to say I now love God liturgically. Love is for persons not things, and Christian love and commitment are not meant to terminate at a 'thing', even a holy thing like the celebration of the liturgy, but should be given to God.

This transition from noun to adverb in religion is an important step in spiritual growth. If I love the liturgy, centre my life upon it, go all out to perfect the parish practice of it, communicate this enthusiasm to others in all seasons, this is not quite the same as loving God liturgically. The enthusiasm I should be communicating to others is an enthusiasm for God, the Father of Jesus Christ our Lord. The liturgy is indeed the ordained way to approach God, but there is a real difference between one who worships the liturgy and one who worships God liturgically. The latter is the mature person who has learnt to distinguish between what is relative and what is Absolute in Christianity.

This distinction is one that needs to be kept in mind, especially today when there is such a rebirth of religious practices in the Church. It is a rebirth which holds great promise for Christian spirituality as long as the need to mature through the noun stage to the adverb stage is remembered. Our parish has people who love the liturgy, the charismatic movement, the Movement for a Better World, the Focolare Movement, the rosary, the Bible, prayer. Our endeavour must be to help them to be people who love God liturgically, charismatically, for a better world, as a family, with the rosary, reading the Bible, praying; committing themselves completely to almighty God, but being flexible and unpossessive about the means used. Many of us can look back to the time when we were totally devoted to some particular form of prayer and pretty rigid in our views and practice of it. It should have helped us to the stage of being totally abandoned to God and flexible with regard to prayer. The use of ladders, after all, is to climb up and not to stay on.

One reason for wanting to pass quickly through the stage of loving religious practices for their own sake is the danger this holds that we may be loving ourselves in disguise. Religious practices are 'things', as I have said, but love is for persons, so when we love a practice like prayer, or a movement in the Church, it could be that we are loving these things as extensions, projections of ourselves. All enthusiasms contain within themselves a hidden egoism. You go on an ego-trip when you go mad about stamps, trains, antiques, etc. You are amassing self-importance as you amass these things. This is no less true of us when we go mad about religion. Initially religious enthusiasm is full of swollen egoism. The injured spouse who takes up spirituality when rejected by the other partner is a case in point. He or she has some way to go before the spiritual enthusiasm is purified of the baser motives of wounded vanity and revenge. In his play about Thomas à Becket, *Murder in the Cathedral*, T. S. Eliot gives Thomas a fourth temptation when he was only expecting three. This fourth temptation was the temptation to be a martyr, not for pure reasons but for reasons of vanity and revenge (i.e. for reasons of projected self-love). From the other side of the grave he would have his revenge on King Henry. This was the temptation to 'do the right deed for the wrong reason'. The human mind has its deviousness, so we should not be surprised to learn that some part of our love for religious practices consists in love of self. In Eliot's play St Thomas reflects sadly,

Servant of God has chance of greater sin
And sorrow, than the man who serves a king.
For those who serve the greater cause may make the cause serve them,
Still doing right.

To be aware of this danger is an important point in the Christian spiritual life. It should urge us to transfer our enthusiasm as quickly as possible away from the various ladders which lead to heaven directly to God himself. Incidentally, the more this happens, the easier we will be to live with. A servant of the lady who, under the influence of St Francis of Sales, became St Jane Frances de Chantal said, 'The first director that Madame had made her pray three times a day, and we were all put out; but Monsieur of Geneva makes her pray all day long, and no one is troubled.'

Prayer and *Aggiornamento*

Catholics have had an opportunity to exercise flexibility with regard to religious forms in the years of *Aggiornamento* since the Vatican Council. The snake has been shedding its old skin and growing a new one. We have all had to recognize that the old skin was only a skin and not the snake itself. We have done this best when prayer has led us to pass beneath the surface of Church life and penetrate to the realms of the spirit. In other words those who have remained on the surface of Catholic practices giving their allegiance to the practices themselves have found *Aggiornamento* hard to take, as the things they thought to be of the essence of Catholicism have been swept away. But those whose devotion penetrated beneath the practices to God himself have been able to live through the changes, upheld by their knowledge that there have been alterations only in the realm of religious practice and that God does not change. I can, after all, love our Father in heaven with equal generosity at a solemn monastic high Mass which evokes the Christian centuries with absolute authenticity and at a noisy youth Mass where the guitars are twanging and nobody keeps still for a minute. In both services my loving Father is present and that is what matters most. The presence of the God, not the man-made apparatus for reaching him, is the focus of worship. The two ladders are totally different, but they both reach to God, even though they start from different places.

There will, of course, always be preferences. He would be a strange person who found himself equally 'at home' at monastic high Mass and a folk celebration. These preferences remain; part of the pastoral task is giving due regard to them and respecting the differences of temperament, background, training which are to be found among people. Alongside these preferences, however, there should be a deepening devotion to the Lord who gave them to us and who wants us to journey beneath the surface accidentals and meet him there.

When contact has been made and prolonged in prayer the emphasis shifts. It shifts away from the different varieties of serving God and concentrates on God himself who is always there and who ultimately is best encountered in the silence and stillness of the heart: that silent still point in the centre of the heart is where God already dwells. We must learn to cultivate contact with God there. When that is done we can confidently participate in the 'outward' activities of the prayer group or the liturgy. Cardinal Newman's motto *Cor ad cor loquitur* – heart speaks to heart – expresses the essence of all worship and Christian activity. By going on the journey inwards and maintaining deep down union with God in all we do, we serve God in a way that would have appealed to the Old Testament prophets with their suspicion of merely external worship. The spiritual worship they and St Paul asked for was a matter of the heart, not of external actions.

The deep prayer of the inward journey enables us to be calm and flexible when it comes to change. A Christian with a healthy life of prayer is almost by definition able to sustain change without panic or bitterness. This is a way of saying that the mature Christian is the one who is not rocked by change because he is anchored to God in prayer. He is, on the contrary, excited by change, because it will, if good, bring God to more people and more people to God.

Chapter Six

INNER AND CENTRE

God's Freedom

In the last chapter I spoke of the discernible shift in emphasis which happens when we find ourselves concentrating more on God than on the means we use for contacting him. As long as we remember the distinctions we made in that last chapter we can call this a shift from religion to faith. Faith does not discard religious practices, but it 'goes through' them to God and therefore treats them flexibly and in the last analysis as provisional. Jesus once said, 'Where your treasure is there your heart will be.' The man of faith knows that his treasure is simply God, so he sets his heart on God. He then finds himself viewing everything less than God, however holy, however necessary, however spiritually exciting, with a healthy freedom. He does not feel bound to one particular form of spiritual approach but feels free to love God in the way that appears best at a given moment. This is the liberated freedom we spoke about in chapter two.

The most important freedom to remember is God's freedom. He is free to treat each person exactly as he likes, free to follow no pattern at all if he so chooses. So we ought not to look for a universal idea of spiritual growth which all must follow. This applies especially to the question of speed in spiritual growth. With some people God acts quickly; they undergo a sudden conversion like a thunderclap; all suddenly is new, astonishing; they feel reborn. But with other people God acts slowly, and their growth towards God is a slow trickle. They never feel reborn but grow imperceptibly both to themselves and to others. They are the conscientious tortoises, not the enthusiastic hares. But, as in the fable, they get to their goal eventually. A sign of spiritual development is recognizing this freedom of God to act as he wants. We learn, when mature, to respect the different ways of Christians and not to expect them to be like ourselves. The twice-born converts learn to esteem the steady, very secure growth of the unspectacular spiritual tortoises, and those tortoises learn to see genuine spirituality in their Road to Damascus brethren and not to be suspicious of sudden, apparently superficial change. In other words we all learn to respect God's controlling influence and to reflect that we ourselves are not in charge of our spiritual lives.

In this chapter I want to look more fully into the liberating shift of emphasis from religion to faith. What follows amounts to a succession of descriptions, describing the same happening in different ways. This is the only way to talk about a rich happening like spiritual conversion. The reader must not think that there is any time sequence involved. This is not a list of progressive steps in spiritual growth. It is not a line, but a circle. Spiritual growth seldom proceeds in a straight line but tends to go round in a circle, returning to the same point over and over again with a wearisome consistency. But each time we go a little deeper, and also come a little closer, so that over the years there is a movement from outer to inner as well as from shallow to deep.

Spiritual Growth

I suppose the most exciting shift in emphasis that takes place in conversion is the discovery that spirituality is a personal relationship. With the best will in the world our first efforts in spirituality tend to be impersonal. We see them as things to do, actions to be performed. In prayer we do use the language of personal relationship, but somehow the attitude we bring to it is impersonal. We relate to the spiritual exercises we do as 'actions' to be performed or 'prayer' to be engaged in. Spirituality is a 'thing'. The only real person in it as yet is ourselves. Then conversion takes place, and suddenly God becomes personal to us! It is no longer an action called prayer we engage in, but God, the Lord, a Person, Him, we relate to. The whole Christian life becomes suffused with this personal presence of God. The spiritual exercises we have always undertaken cease in our mind to be things to be done. They become means of loving the Lord, pleasing him. We come to realize that the whole of our everyday life can be lived in a relationship with Jesus Christ. He becomes a companion in the things we do. We enter into conversation with him, not only in prayer, but also in the actions of our life: they become ways of contacting God, 'words' we use to converse with him. It is an exciting change. Martin Buber would say that we have moved in our attitude towards God from I-it to I-Thou. It is the beginning of a personal interior life.

In the realm of conduct there is a similar shift in emphasis. At the initial impersonal stage religion is conduct-centred. Our Christian response is seen very much in terms of morality, of doing good and avoiding evil. The active aspect of the gospel looms large and our approach to it is severely practical. This is true both of old-fashioned Christians with an individualistic understanding of their religion ('What must I do to be saved?') and also of modern Christians. They, too, show themselves to be conduct-centred in their overriding concerns for the social gospel and a new ethic of political awareness. Since the Vatican Council the content of much religious writing has changed from concern with problems of personal salvation to concern with the problems of mankind, like justice and peace and human rights. It is a welcome change because it means that Christians are becoming seriously involved in the world they belong to and want to make it a better place. By itself, however, it represents no great growth in maturity. These Christians still see their religion moralistically, in terms of sorting out human actions and applying the principles of the gospel to them. They are fundamentally ethical in their approach. New radical is often old moralist writ large. At this stage prayer is, of course, not forgotten, but it is seen as a means of becoming good, of reforming our actions. We pray in order to be better persons. We pray for the grace to be good, pure, charitable, honest (old emphasis), or the grace to set in motion an effective programme of social-political action (new emphasis). Prayer at this stage has a habit of ending in resolutions. It is not all that open-ended.

With conversion this alters. From being an auxiliary to conduct, prayer now becomes central – the whole of the Christian response, in fact. My life simply becomes prayer, not in the sense that I am on my knees all day, but in the sense of that continual conversation with the Lord. My actions, the conduct of my life, appear in my mind as a series of ways of pleasing God. It is no longer easy to view one's conduct impersonally as actions to be done for specific purposes. It is much easier, and more real, to see them as part of one's approach to Jesus our Lord, successive words in one's conversation with him. I live my life now under the inspiration of the Holy Spirit, in partnership with Jesus, so what I do is part of that partnership. 'The right relationship between prayer and conduct is not that conduct is supremely important and prayer helps it, but that prayer is supremely important and conduct is its test' (William Temple). One sees now the truth of that statement.

This 'personalization' of conduct has an interesting psychological result. In our minds, the Christian virtues coalesce into one, namely, love. As long as we are seeing Christianity in terms of deeds to be done, then we have to draw up lists of virtues to be acquired and vices to be eradicated. The tasks we address ourselves to are varied: tasks in the field of justice, of family love, of personal purity, and so on. Each one is different from the others, so the list of virtues and vices is long in order to cover all circumstances, especially when we take into account the problems of political theology and human rights as well as individual living. But when Christianity simplifies for us into a matter of pleasing God, then our approach to it coalesces into that simple task of loving God in all the situations of life. The situations we find ourselves in are as many and varied as before, but our response now does not vary. It remains the inner one of love. We keep the list of ethical precepts for the sake of planning and education, but we now view it as a list of exciting opportunities for exercising love. In politics loving God will take the form of acting justly; at home it will be called family love; in some acute personal situations it will be purity. These virtues may have different names but inwardly they are one and the same, being exercises of love. In all cases unless there is love of God there will be no virtue, however impressive the programme. This is the theme of the thirteenth chapter of St Paul's first Epistle to the Corinthians. St Paul outlines a very diverse list of Christian responses ranging from the exercise of charismatic gifts to the works of mercy; but he does so in order to point out that they are merely exercises in Christian love, and if that is absent the external actions simply count for nothing. Another famous saying on this subject is St Augustine's 'Love God and do what you will.' Because they stem from my love of God my actions are virtues. There is no need to draw up long lists of virtuous actions to be performed. Concentrate on loving surrender to God, and they will happen automatically.

When she was a young girl at home St Thérèse of Lisieux was taught by her elder sisters to keep a daily list of her actions of self-denial. The idea was that by keeping this continual tally she would build up virtue and eradicate sins and imperfections. When she went from home to the Carmelite convent her novice-mistress encouraged her to continue the practice. Thérèse, however, was a clear-sighted person and she soon saw how artificial and how self-centred this practice was. So she abandoned it. Instead she decided to make her aim in life that of 'pleasing Jesus'. The lists of good deeds were put away and a loving attention to our Lord took their place. Thérèse turned to God her Father in utter trust and love. She did not want to build up virtue or acquire merit. She simply wanted to trust God and do his will for his own sake, not for her gain. She hoped when she died to appear 'empty-handed' before God, relying on no merit at all. This courageous launching forth was the beginning of her Little Way. It marked for Thérèse, and for all those who follow her, a notable step in the transition from reliance on the works of religion to the simplicity of faith.

If we consider St Thérèse further, we notice that as she drew near to God she saw herself in the light of God's goodness as full of imperfections. This helped her to stop thinking of her life as a process of building up, acquiring perfection, amassing a record of good conduct. Instead, it appeared to her as a painful process of being stripped down, demolished, made to see how imperfect she was – the very opposite to the former process of building up merit and self-esteem. She was no longer the precociously virtuous centre of attention which she had been in the family when she was her father's favourite and 'Princess'. Instead, she was a rather imperfect young nun, often forgotten and, when noticed, coming under criticism from her prioress. It was undoubtedly a shock to her, but, because of her courage, it was also the occasion for her to redouble her trust and love in God ('*confiance et amour*'). She grew intensely close to God her Father in the self-surrender of love.

The process for St Thérèse was the paradoxical one that the more she saw her faults the closer she went to God, and the closer she went to God the worse her imperfections appeared. This process will be the same for us as we make the transition from religion to faith. While prayer is impersonal we are in no danger of being stripped naked. Once, however, it becomes personal, a direct contact with God, the stripping process begins, because we begin to undergo an encounter with the All Holy. To the degree that this meeting is real, it wiil be a demolishing one. Put

73

briefly, while we are the centre of our own attention, we experience only a sense of building up, a sense of spiritual achievement. But when our life becomes a personal dialogue, with *God* the other end of that dialogue, then our sense of achievement collapses like a house of cards. In comparison with the All Holy we know that we are nothing, 'a worm and no man', as the psalmist puts it. Few of us relish this, because it involves painful loss of self-esteem. The sight of self as prone to evil, emptily selfish, vain is not pleasant. Instead of being built up, we are torn down, left with no cosy feeling of spiritual well-being.

It is hard to realize that this demolition process in our Christian life is a step forward, because it feels like ten steps backward. We therefore need the trust and love which St Thérèse made central to her Little Way. Jesus' parable of the Pharisee and the Publican at prayer should convince us of this need. The Pharisee was a good man, but his spirituality was still at the 'outer' stage. He spent his time listing his virtues, acquired through God's help. The publican had moved to an 'inner' position where he knew he had to rely wholly on God's mercy not on his own achievements. He knew himself to be sinful, as he threw himself in trust and love on the mercy of God.

Trust and love are both the chicken and the egg in this process of spiritual growth. At first they are the way in which I contact God directly and so bring upon me the painful sight of myself as sinful and far from perfection. Then from the midst of the despair brought on by this impact of truth, trust and love are the response I make to God, the only possible way out of the situation: Lord, be merciful to me a sinner. I melt into God in trust and love; he only is my 'refuge'. This direct contact with God results in a new cycle of despair, as God reveals a little more of my rottenness to me, and I reply with deeper trust and love. And so the process goes on, continually spiralling down on the journey inwards. As the spiral continues, however, sadness is left behind, discarded at the surface with one's self-esteem and spiritual ambitions. Deep down one learns to let go into God with more and more joy. One is increasingly unconcerned about God's gifts towards oneself, because one is possessed by God. 'You have written well of me. What reward would you like to have?' was the voice St Thomas Aquinas heard speaking from the crucifix. His reply was, 'No reward but you yourself, Lord.' Not the gifts but the Giver was his desire.

Copernican Revolution

One of the features of parish liturgy today is the number of special Sundays we are expected to observe in the course of the year. We have Vocations Sunday, Catholic Education Sunday, Lay Apostolate Sunday, Communications Sunday and so on. Each Sunday produces its own liturgy and special sermon. If this trend continues we may soon have an alternative liturgical cycle for the Sundays of the year. The old liturgical cycle based on the objective mystery of Christ's redemption will have given way to a new cycle based on the subjective needs of Church and world. Should this happen it will be a case of subjective spirituality taking over from an objective spirituality. Often, when giving retreats, I am asked to prepare a liturgy of joy, or penance, or celebration, or some other human response appropriate for the retreat. I try to resist these requests, because I think liturgy is meant to centre round what Jesus Christ did for mankind, not round the response made to him by mankind. So I resist the urge for subjective celebration and try to get back to objective liturgies of transfiguration, passion and death, resurrection, ascension, pentecost. In practice these liturgies turn out to be ones of joy, penance, celebration, thanksgiving, but they do so by focussing our attention upon Jesus Christ and not upon ourselves.

The danger of congregation-centred liturgies is that they engender a self-centred spirituality in us all. Our main concern becomes ourselves rather than God. We desire to make God work for us instead of surrendering ourselves to him. We desire to control God. There will in fact be no conversion if we do not resist this move towards a spirituality of harnessing God to our needs. Such a spirituality increases the preoccupation we have over our lives to such an extent that we become absorbed in our selves and needs. Inevitably this is how we begin our spiritual journey. The desire to be in control is the point of departure. We plan a spiritual programme for ourselves. We set out to put it into action, sitting at the controls like the pilot of an aeroplane. At this stage God is little more than an element in our spiritual life. He is not yet in any real sense a person to us. We are preoccupied still with our spiritual responses, not yet with God. Conversion, however, is that moment when we bump up against God almost for the first time as a real person. We then realize that we are not in control, God is. From then on the spiritual journey becomes a matter of letting go, not of holding tight. It is a reversal of our expectations and, of course, does not happen overnight. Sooner or later, however, it has to happen if we are to advance close to God. Advancing close to God means accepting reality. Reality is the fact that God is Creator and we are creatures, that God is Saviour and we are saved. We do not see this until with our whole being we have lived through the experience of loss of control over our own spiritual programme.

The experience of conversion, when we pass from 'outer' religion to 'inner' faith often begins with a radical experience of incompetence. This is God's way of making us let go. In a mysterious way all our previous competence in spiritual matters fades away and we are left with the painful realization of our mediocrity. Methods of prayer tend to break down and no longer produce results. Likewise our programmes for Christian action get shattered. What seemed obvious and easy when we first began seems ineffectual now. The systems no longer work. The important element at this stage is how we respond to this humiliating discovery of incompetence before God. One could list a variety of mistaken reactions to this experience, ranging from resolute non-acceptance of the fact to bewildered despair. The only effective reaction is the one St Thérèse (and all the saints) made; namely, a redoubling of trust and love of God. It is both the simplest reaction and also for most of us the hardest. It is not easy to surrender to God. It is, of course, easy for me to write about complete surrender to God in the midst of incompetence. The words pour fluently on to the page. But in practice this abandonment, this letting go into God's hands is just plain difficult. It is difficult because human beings do not find it easy to relinquish control over their affairs when their education has in fact been in the direction of establishing control. But if at the proper time they do not let go they will never pass over to an objective spiritual life but will remain closed in their subjectivity. The experience of incompetence in the practice of one's spiritual life is, therefore, the breakthrough to Christian maturity. Through this experience God draws us to the life of loving him, away from preoccupation with self and into a life of wonder and adoration in which we become lost in God.

This spiritual breakthrough, or liberation, into maturity can aptly be called a copernican revolution in one's spirituality. In the sixteenth century, Copernicus discovered that contrary to appearances the sun did not go round the earth but the earth went round the sun. Something similar happens to us when as a result of our spiritual incompetence we let go into God. Hitherto, following appearances, we have thought ourselves to be the centre of our own world. Firmly in control, we have 'occupied' the centre of our religious life. From this stronghold we have, as it were, admitted God into our world and given the recognition due to him. We have stayed at the centre and worshipped God 'out there' at the circumference. Then comes the dismal experience of sinfulness and incompetence when our spiritual achievements collapse about us and, like the publican in the parable, we bow our heads in a plea for mercy. God answers our prayer with an insight into truth, which comes to us in the midst of our humiliation. It dawns on us that God is not in our world; we are in his! He is the Creator who has created us and put us in his world. He is, in other words, the central point of the universe, and it is we who are at the circumference, revolving round him. The former impression that we were in the centre, in charge of our spiritual life is now seen as false, as false as the ancient view that the earth was the centre of the universe, with the sun, stars and moon circling round it. We realize with a liberating joy that God is the central point, and prayer for us becomes simply recognizing this and adoring him in wonder.

Many further things could be said about the copernican revolution in our souls. It is a breakthrough into truth: until we realize that God is in the centre drawing us towards him we are seeing things to a certain extent falsely. It is also a breakthrough into maturity: how immature it is, to imagine ourselves to be allotting a place for God in our lives, judging that he is relevant to our world – he who creates and goes on creating the world all the time. It is also a breakthrough into passivity in Christian living. We cease to be active and grasping in our approach to God and learn at least to yield to him and allow him to grasp us. We relinquish the primordial grip we have on our lives and surrender to God. The poet's 'Thou mastering me, God' sums up our new response. Instead of trying to master the Almighty we let him master us. It is strange how long it takes for most of us to learn this lesson.

This spiritual breakthrough into sheer wonder and adoration of God is the final stage of the journey inwards. As we journey interiorly we leave behind our dependence upon the works of religion. We stop trying to build up a spiritual position for ourselves, stop viewing God merely as a source of spiritual benefits. Those attitudes belong to the outer surface of life. Travelling inwards to God, who dwells in our hearts but is the centre of creation, we are turned inside out. Turning inwards we face God in the depths of our being and are emptied of spiritual acquisitiveness. In our poverty we sink and merge into the utter richness of God. We, as it were, melt into the Godhead, and if we have any thoughts and feelings they are of sheer wonder at the astonishing holiness of God. In this holy fullness we drown as in an unfathomable sea. The terminus of the journey inwards is, then, this merging into God in a union of wonder. The psalmist sang, 'I will sing for ever of your love, O Lord.' This ceaseless song goes on in our hearts whatever we are doing. Once we have entered upon union with God in our hearts both the journey outwards and the journey inwards become an endless song of wonder. It does not matter what we are doing. All gives glory to God. Our whole life sings to God of his glory because we have let go inside ourselves.

Chapter Seven

THE JOURNEY OUTWARDS

The quotation from St Ambrose at the head of this book takes two well-known New Testament injunctions on prayer which appear to say opposite things and joins them together. Jesus told us to go to our rooms in private when we want to pray. St Paul told us to pray everywhere. A contradiction? Probably so, but we need not worry, because New Testament sayings are not meant to dovetail perfectly. They are not commands for all Christians on all occasions. The simplest response to these two sayings is to note that they are pieces of advice to separate audiences on separate occasions. Jesus and Paul are talking about two different kinds of praying to two different kinds of people; hence the contradiction. Nevertheless St Ambrose's linking of St Paul's recommendation to pray everywhere with Jesus' advice to go into an inner closet to pray is interesting, because it echoes the theme of this book: that we must find a cloister for our prayer and Christian life, but that that cloister should not be a physical one, separating us from people, but the cloister of a recollected heart. While remaining completely in this world and going about our business in it, we must go on the journey inwards to the divine Presence dwelling in our hearts. This sort of cloister is the fundamental one of Christianity. It fulfilled in New Testament times the spirituality of the prophets of the Old Testament who called for an internal covenant of the heart and a law written in the inmost being of God's people. It creates a spirituality which is suitable for the twentieth century, especially for those living in a modern city parish. In this chapter I offer some sketches to illustrate that fact.

Open House

Some priests today turn the houses they live in into open houses where all and sundry can come in and use the place as their own with the active encouragement of the priests. University chaplains have been doing this for some time. The practice has spread to priests working in parishes. Our own parish does this. We do not lock the front door and anyone may enter who cares. The result is an intermittent stream of people through the house, especially young people who use the place as a youth centre. We have no parish hall but we have this big house, with one room which holds seventy people and others (our own rooms) which take a dozen or more. There is also the dining-room with television and the spacious kitchen. These two rooms are occupied more than any others as rooms where people can come not to seek an interview with a priest or for a meeting, but just to sit and chat, make a cup of tea, watch television, enjoy themselves. In effect the house is the parish centre where all meetings except very big ones take place, with this important qualification: that it is also the house the priests live in, in other words their home which they share with those who come in. Among these are people we have staying with us to whom we have given a bed for some reason or other. They share in our life while they are with us, whether they are bishops or tramps.

The idea behind this practice of having an open

house is to make the house the priests live in the chief instrument of their apostolate. It seems a pity to exclude the parish house from the work of the parish apostolate if, with a bit of generosity, the two areas can be merged. Once it is accepted that the house is itself in the front line of the battle and not a rest centre behind the lines, then the work of the apostolate expands considerably. With the merging of the two spheres private and public, there comes an equivalent merging of private and public times in a priest's life. Not only his work, but also his relaxation, his eating, and even his praying become shared with the people. In other words, as we said above, the priests' house becomes an instrument of the work they do. They do not emerge from a private, slightly fortified residence to do their work in other people's homes only. By opening their own house, they can go on doing their work at home as well as abroad. Instead of living a kind of double life with only the public part shared with the parishioners they can live a unified life liable to be spent with others at any time, but also, of course, liable to be spent alone at any time too. An open house is not packed with people twenty-four hours a day. Nor is it always noisy. A room by the front door in our house is a small chapel, with the Blessed Sacrament. People make visits there, coming in from the street to be quiet before the Lord. We also celebrate the two daily parish Masses in our big upper room, and there too a profound silence reigns and spreads to the rest of the house. This is the time I best experience that merging of public and private lives into one, which is so fruitful for the apostolate.

Built into the concept of priesthood is the idea of availability. The priest is the available man, the man who is exposed to God on behalf of mankind and exposed to men on behalf of God, the man in the middle. This is his liturgical function: to stand at the altar and lectern and be the mediator. A priest's pastoral work flows from this liturgical position. He is the mediator outside liturgy too. He must be available to people, therefore, in life, before and after Mass, in order that at Mass he exercise his priesthood 'really' as well as ritually. Maintaining an open house is one way of ensuring availability to people. The open house system is simply an extension of the availability to their people that priests in these islands have traditionally practised. It goes further than most by abolishing the barriers of door-bell, housekeeper and waiting-room, which undoubtedly daunt many callers, especially the timid ones, and make them postpone or cancel meetings with their pastors. The very nature of the business between pastors and people often makes for shyness and timidity. It is a pity when priests' houses increase rather than lessen the tension already present. Priests with an open house discover that confidences from people in trouble come more easily in their own personal rooms, or just watching television, or washing up together. To be accepted into the family and invited to join in what is going on helps people to trust and risk a confidence in a way that a formal interview with the priest summoned to the parlour does not.

As a priest I am frequently bothered by the question of poverty. We serve a Master who chose an itinerant life, had nowhere to lay his head, and lived a life which was in many respects the opposite to the life of the Catholic clergy in Britain today. Our life is comparatively rich, at least in city parishes. His life was poor. Faced with this contrast some today are so ashamed of the comfortable life of the clergy that they opt to go and live with poor people as poor persons.

I admire their decision. My own solution is to stay in the big house, keep our parish cars, maintain a certain middle-class standard of living, but share it with as many people as possible. For me Christianity means 'sharing' more than any other concept like renunciation, selling all, etc. This may well be less generous than other responses to the gospel, but it seems realistic. There is an advantage in having a house with big rooms, spare bedrooms, a large kitchen. The advantage emerges when these facilities are shared without cost with those who want them. For us, then, poverty means sharing.

With sharing comes joy. As we saw in chapter two, it is not until one has let go of one's anxious, possessive instincts that one experiences true joy. Living in an open house teaches those who do it the deep happiness that comes from a life free of those anxiety-causing elements: precious possessions, guarded privacy, respectability, class barriers. Those who have lived in the liberated atmosphere of a shared house would find it very difficult to go back to the mini-monastery of the traditional priests' house with resident housekeeper, fixed mealtimes, barriers against the public, and the inevitable dichotomy between public and private lives. In spite of the occasional irritations of the open house caused by lack of privacy or things going missing, one would not want to retreat into a protected life, chiefly because of the joy that comes with open living. Genuine exposure to God in prayer and to people in love is the path to happiness for men. The open house is structured to point towards that happiness.

Living in an open house makes a Catholic priest's celibacy more convincing. I am not here discussing the obligatory linking of priesthood and celibacy, but merely commenting on the present celibacy of Catholic priests, a celibacy which will always exist in some numbers. Celibacy has many advantages. A disadvantage is that priestly celibates can so easily become privileged bachelors, protected from the inconveniences of life. Married people live an interrupted life. At all ages their children inconvenience them by day and by night. It would not be right if the life of the pastor were more cushioned against that sort of thing than those of his parishioners. I try to remember this when I occasionally feel irritated by the noise, the untidiness, the mess of living in a house which is also a centre for people, especially the misfits and inadequates of society. I was called to be celibate in order not to be more sheltered than my married contemporaries, but to be more exposed. I gave up the privilege of a family of my own in order to be more available to more people and in order to be able to live in situations which it would not be fair to ask a man with a wife and family to take on. So if at times life in our house becomes noisy and crowded, then I am glad it is our celibacy which has enabled this to be. When people call me 'Father' I like to have earned that title by acting as father to a large family, and not to have been given it on the cheap, with a self-indulgent, closed life-style.

I am not here advocating that priests should have no time off and be perpetually on duty. Time off and away from the job is important for anyone who works with people, especially people in need asking for help. To pretend that one does not need any time away from people would be so to misunderstand one's own human person that one could scarcely be trusted to help another. Nevertheless priesthood calls for more availability than any other calling, and the shared house is an effective means of exercising it. Clearly what is called for is an attitude of mind which enables the pastor to be relaxed as he works. Relaxation in its most important sense is not a thing you do so much as a way you do things. Christians are not only called to do something called relaxation, but to be relaxed in the Lord in everything they do. In other words simultaneously with the journey outwards to things and people, we should be going on the journey inwards to God in the ground of our being. Even as we conduct our interviews, make telephone calls, prepare meals, we can be letting go into God in the deep centre of our beings. There are not two operations – a journey inwards so as to relax followed by a journey outwards to work – but a single one consisting of a more or less vigorous external action which contains an inner element of utter passivity to the will of God. Outwardly there may be much activity, as there so often was in the lives of the saints, but inwardly it is all calm as the soul melts into the being of God. The cloister ensuring peace and calm is not an external one of bricks and mortar but the internalized one of a soul surrendered to God. The Christian who has thus let go to God completely in his heart is able to be effective in the uncloistered secular situations of twentieth-century urban life. Because of this inner adoration he is all glorious within in the far-from-glorious outward circumstances of life.

Team Ministry

Another change that is taking place in parish life is the substitution of a team ministry for the traditional undiversified system of parish priest and curate(s). In many parishes today you are likely to find a variegated team exercising the apostolate. The core team of our parish consists of three priests, a religious sister who is a trained social worker, and a young layman who is a trained teacher with a degree in theology. All work full-time in the parish and work together as a team. The most important effect of having a diversity of persons in the parish team is that the work of the apostolate is correspondingly diversified. Richer results are obtained by a group which has women as well as men, lay people as well as ordained, young, middle-aged and old, living and working together. The wider the range of talents in the parish team the wider the impact of their apostolate. A community of persons, fired with enthusiasm for the same ideal but each interpreting the ideal with his or her own emphasis and, furthermore, each transmitting his interpretation in a unique way because of background, temperament and past experience, produces a richer effect than a couple of priests by themselves.

The core of a parish is its full-time workers. If these live and work together as a team they have the effect of encouraging teamwork among the part-time workers in the parish. By part-time workers I do not mean part-time Christians, but fully committed Christians who find that part of their hundred per cent commitment to Christ is to work outside their families for the community or the parish. From these will come the parish council with its various subcommittees for social life, welfare work, education, ecumenical, liturgical, financial, ethical matters. It is a fact that if the core workers in a parish are trying to work together as a team, their ideals will spread in ever-widening circles out into the parish and encourage teamwork there too. Sharing is infectious. A priest who lives by himself and clings to being sole pastor in the parish finds difficulty in sharing the apostolate with the non-ordained, but priests who readily share responsibility with others attract an ever-increasing number of co-workers to them. People flock to help because they feel welcomed and find it exciting to join in. The more full-time pastors there are in a parish the more the parishioners will want to join in the work and so produce a multiplicity of effort. Nothing succeeds like success. This incidentally is the chief factor in making for an open house with much going on in it. A lively parish just cannot be kept out.

A prerequisite for this teamwork in a parish is that each respects the insights, talents and achievements of the others in the team. We all tend to go off at tangents in our work and no one person's tangent is exactly the same as another's. Christianity is a unified ideal, but it is rich enough to produce many such tangential interpretations, each of which is Christian but none of which represents the whole of Christianity. I am not thinking of the diversity of work produced by the fact that the average parish contains a variety of people ranging from old to young, from sick to healthy, from rich to poor, and from fervent to lapsed. Those age-old varieties clearly diversify the work from the start. The tangents I have in mind are the tangents of our enthusiasms.

The more committed and enthusiastic a parish worker is the more he will be fired by an ideal. In this fertile period of post-Vatican-ii church life there are many ideals coming to birth. Movements abound like the Focolare Movement, Charismatic Movement, Better World Movement, Encounter Movement. They have each a particular ideal to offer. The open parish will welcome them and encourage them to flourish. Usually different members of a parish team will promote them and make them his or her own particular 'thing'. Hence the need for mutual respect for others' enthusiasms and a firm control over the old Adam in each of us to see that going off at our own particular tangent does not make us blind or unsympathetic towards those of others. This is the problem of unity in diversity which is as old as Christianity, as readers of the First Epistle to the Corinthians know. One way to solve the problem is to have no parish activity and hence no parish tensions. This is, however, the way of death. The Christian ideal is to have ever-increasing life with more and more tangents to go off at, coupled with genuine sympathy for the enthusiasms of others. If this respect is genuine it will lead to the logical conclusion by each movement that it is not the whole of Christianity but only a part. This is never easy for enthusiastic persons to see, but the seeing of it makes the difference between true catholicity and sectarianism. We have to love enough to allow other people to be different from ourselves. In practice allowing others to differ from us is our test to ensure that we serve the great Cause and do not manipulate the Cause to serve us. Mixed in with most enthusiasms is our rooted egoism. It has to be weeded out so as to prevent us from trampling on other people in the name of religious zeal. We have to learn the hard lesson that ideals are optional because men are free, and that they can only be offered to other people, not forced upon them. Genuine love means giving people freedom, even the painful freedom to reject us. Practising this genuine love is the way we kill our native egoism. I believe that Christians only attempt to do this if they have a life of deep prayer, the sort of prayer which penetrates below the surface differences to contact the One Lord underlying them all, and have learned to go on trusting him, because

90

God's ways are not man's ways, and God's thoughts are not man's thoughts.

A second prerequisite for good teamwork in a parish is that there be open and honest communication between the members so that everyone knows what each member is doing and is not left to feel insecure, through ignorance of what is being planned. This requires strong and tactful leadership from the centre and a certain structure of communication (fixed meetings, etc.). Most teams, however, communicate best informally and in an unplanned way. In our house we sometimes find ourselves together in the kitchen near midnight making a cup of tea and spontaneously a planning session or a serious pastoral discussion occurs. It happens late at night because so often by day we go our own ways and scarcely meet. It is not wise, however, to leave all communication to happen spontaneously. Fixed meetings and planning sessions are also necessary, especially those planning sessions which look backwards in assessment and forwards in the long term and are not merely concerned with what we shall do next week. It goes without saying that the essential element in communication is internal, a condition of the heart which clears away our fears and makes us ready to be open, honest, flexible with each other. In this respect, we have found it helpful in our team to have a session of prayer together on Saturday nights in which we share our plans for the parish at the important level of laying them before God. We have found truth in the old saying that the family that prays together stays together, in both work and fellowship.

Leadership in the Church at all levels requires trust. The person who is called to leadership must have learned to know his fears and how to handle them. We all have fears. There is no such person as the fearless man. Often we can live for years without knowing our fears. In a quiet, unobtrusive life they can be muted. Being placed in a position of leadership is one of the ways our fears rise to the surface and begin to bother us where before they were scarcely felt. A common way of dealing with fear is by mistrust. It happens almost automatically with no conscious decision. I find myself threatened by a person or by a developing situation and immediately manifest distrust. I am tempted to panic either by running away or by aggression. This is the important moment of decision. If I do nothing about my feelings of fear I will have passed into a state of conscious, chosen distrust. But if I try to conquer my fears, however feebly, I will be a courageous man. The brave person is not the (non-existent) fearless person, but the one who sets out to conquer fear by positive steps. Often these steps are small ones like going to talk to someone who frightens me; forgiving a neighbour who has hurt me; reading a book or article which fills me with panic; asking a permission when tempted to presume it. Such small acts of courage make for love and unity in a group. If we avoid them the small fissures in society become large ones. Soon the gap between people has become a yawning one, and it needs a much more courageous approach to try to close it. Very few people who have funked the initial small act of courage can summon up enough bravery to make the later big one. Thus fear drives out love in a community.

Leadership at all levels in the Church today has to face this problem of fear spilling over into mistrust. At the parish level in which I work I am aware of fears inside me. The unknown and the untried make me suspicious and sometimes frankly frightened. It is so much easier to resist new ideas and practices, because then there will be no risk of things being changed, and so no necessity to readjust my thinking and the tried way of the parish. It is also easy to call this resistance by the dishonest name of prudence. But that resistance is cowardly and leads to death in any community, especially a Catholic parish with its built-in conservatism. I know that I must constantly expose myself and the parish to new ways. One of the fears which dwells in us is the fear that things will get out of control. This fear makes us want to control everything ourselves and prevents us from delegating tasks to others. We grip tight to all that happens and do not allow initiative in others. I recognize this fear in myself and observe that I am often willing to entertain new ideas if they arise in my own mind, but am distrustful of new ideas which come from others, especially when those others are younger. There is jealousy involved here too, jealousy inspired by fear and weakness.

The good leader will face these fears in himself and drive them out with trust and love. He learns to let go inside himself and leave his worries in God's hands. He must *really* believe that God guides his Church and that the Holy Spirit has been released among Christians to sustain them and help them to build God's Kingdom. This happy and untroubled trust emanating from the leader catches on and makes the community first secure and then adventurous. An anxious leader filled with fears makes his followers fearful too and kills the spirit of experiment and adventure. Experiment and adventure and risk (all values from the gospel) flourish when the community has been inspired to let go, be free, relax, give glory to God, and allow the Holy Spirit to work in its midst.

Two things help us to let go in our responsibilities.

At the surface level living in an open house makes us relax and give glory to God because of the sheer uncontrollability of the situation. When the house fills up with guitars in one room, meetings in another, and tramps in the kitchen, we realize that we cannot possibly control what happens, or be fussy and over-tidy, so we have to let go into the arms of God and exercise our responsibilities through him. It is his house and his children who come and go in it, so it is up to him to watch over what happens and give signs to us as to how to behave. At the deeper level the journey inwards in prayer to complete fusion with God in the depths involves the most important letting go of all and inspires all the other surface surrenders. If I am surrendered in my heart to God I can live joyfully in the crazy present and face the foreboding future with serenity. God, I realize, is in charge and in my heart I am joined to him. So I need not worry. This sort of leadership aims at being an enabler, giving people plenty of space to be themselves and think their own thoughts. It is not an abdication of responsibility but a recognition that true responsibility lies with God, and the leader's responsibility is to subordinate to that and not to play the emperor himself. Naturally such a course involves self-discipline and brings some suffering, because freedom allows evil to flourish alongside good. Threatening things will happen in an open community because the devil sows tares among the wheat. This calls for the suffering of the servant leader who at the centre should take the strain without complaint, and so enable the community to expand and be joyful. By his wounds and hurts the leader enables the community to grow. This would be a crazy way of doing things if Jesus Christ had not done it first and shown the way to us. Christ was a king, but the crown he wore was a crown of thorns. His followers need not expect any different treatment.

Parish Community

Many today question the value of the residential parish, the parish based on a geographical area. They would like to see the parish system, at least in cities, replaced by something more dynamic and suited to the social mobility of people today. They question whether you can form a community in any valuable sense among people in a modern city. City dwellers live side by side but do not mix, make their friends on quite another basis than the street they live in, and already belong to many different social groupings based on work, common interests, special callings. I have sympathy with this viewpoint but think, nevertheless, that you can form a community in any place where people have houses to live in, because the relationships formed by living side by side in a locality are, in fact, more stable and tangible than any others. There is a potentiality in them that you do not get in other relationships.

A city parish today is different from past parochial communities. We have to remember this and resist the temptation to compare it with the closer, homogeneous parishes of the past, especially those of our childhood. To begin with, there is the fact, already mentioned, that individuals in a parish belong to a variety of other communities besides that of the parish. Their friends, their work, their hobbies, their sporting activities, their age groups provide other groupings to belong to than the parish. A parish 'social', for instance, is only one of many social gatherings a parishioner can go to, and there is no reason why it should demand a special loyalty. This is a change from the recent past when 'the Parish' was the primary, and sometimes the only, community that Catholics belonged to. The modern city parish is an altogether looser grouping than it was in the past. Gone are the days of the tightly-knit community, providing all social as well as liturgical life for its members. Gone with that concept is the old type 'P.P.' who presided over this community in an appropriately tight-knit way.

A second reason why the modern parish is a looser grouping than it used to be is that its own activities are more variegated than before. It has many sub-groups. Bible-study groups, prayer groups, third world groups, discussion groups, apostolic organizations, youth activity, social clubs of different kinds exist side by side in the parish and serve to build the parish into a confederation of activities. It becomes almost like a diocese holding together a plurality of different spiritual entities and less like the uniform parish of the past. In our own parish, as the activities grew we received complaints from older parishioners that too much was going on in the parish and that they could not keep pace with it all. This puzzled us until we realized that they were assuming that, as loyal parishioners, they ought to belong to all the groups and support every activity that was launched. We were able to point out that this was neither desirable nor possible. Everyone learnt a lesson when it was realized that new activities in the parish (*another* discussion group, *another* service in the church) did not mean one more summons for the loyal support but could be guiltlessly passed by and left to others. We came to accept that the parish today is a mixture of varied activities and groups and no one person, priest or lay, could be in everything. Along with this acceptance comes a realization of the importance of a strong parish council which can co-ordinate these activities and keep the lines of communication open between all the groups. We have found that our parish council only occasionally initiates action from the top or undertakes action as a body. More often it acts as a clearing-house for information and guidance among its sub-groups, which are themselves busy and active with their own initiatives. The activities of the parish tend to take place in the smaller gatherings 'out at the circumference', and the work at the centre is a holding operation of support, guidance, letting be. Parish councillors, along with the priests, learn in the modern parish not to be too dominant or clerical. They learn to serve rather than rule the widely diverse collection of communities which make up the parish.

These two understandings about modern parish life, which recognize that the parish is only one among many communities which its members belong to, and which ensure that within the parish community individuals find smaller sub-groups to join, lead me to argue for the value of the parish system in today's society. The lesson that the parish as opposed to other groups has to teach us is the lesson of discipleship and the lesson of grace: that we did not choose Jesus Christ, he chose us. The parish system says to us: by all means select your particular Christian interest, join a prayer group, discussion group, apostolic organization, and grow as a disciple of Christ in that group; feel free, too, to leave the group if you find it is not for you. But remember, also, that you are called to belong to a parish where you are not free to choose but instead have been chosen. In the parish, at Mass, you are not free to choose whom to love and associate with, but are asked to exchange the kiss of peace with

97

your neighbour – and if you do not like him, or feel inhibited because he is of a different class, or colour, or age or appearance, then so much the better for your Christian practice! The value of the parish system is precisely that it cuts across our natural desire to flock with birds of the same feather, takes us out of our inborn cliquishness and does not allow us carefully to select the neighbour with whom we will religiously consort. The more we have smaller Christian groups to nurture like-minded people at the personal level, the more necessary it is to have a strong parish community which attempts to weld together disparate types in living worship. The modern parish tries to serve both interests. By encouraging small groups it encourages the growth that can only take place in the fellowship of similarly inspired enthusiasts. By being a parish (chosen for me) and not just a congregation (chosen by me), it encourages growth in the most important areas of all: charity, humility, forgiveness, tolerance. I am reminded of the titled lady who, when the vernacular liturgy was introduced, came to say she could not stand 'those dreadful Irish voices' all round her, so went to the university chaplaincy where she found comfort in their cultured worship. I sympathized (a bit) with her. But was she not failing an important fence and missing an opportunity of growth by her self-indulgent evasion?

The fact that the parish is not just for those who choose it but for all within its bounds makes it what Rosemary Haughton has called a Formation Community as opposed to a Transformed Community. Transformed Communities are societies of people who have all undergone a transforming religious experience and feel spiritually reborn. Consequently the group they form has an underlying assumption that the highest standards are possible and makes its rules accordingly. They are strict and demanding. Its prayer will be enthusiastic, even extravagant, explicitly aspiring to sanctity. One thinks of the early Franciscans, the sects of the seventeenth century, or of charismatic groups today, and of prayers like this: 'Spirit of the living God, fall afresh on me. Melt me, mould me, fill me, use me.' A Formation Community, on the other hand, is a community which is on the way to sanctity but is made up of many who have made very little progress that way. Its entry standards are about as low as they can be. It takes in anyone who is available to join and makes no demands about achievement, only about desire. Consequently the way of life of such a group is full of 'scandals' as well as noble effort, and its prayers will be deliberately unexplicit and seemingly neutral so that they can be recited at many different spiritual levels by the variety of worshippers. One thinks of the prayers Sunday after Sunday in the Roman Missal which are content to ask for generalized things like health and salvation, leaving it to each individual in the community to place his own explicit meaning on the corporate petition. Formation Communities have to be general in their statements because of the wide 'scatter' in understanding and discipleship among their members. They have to be tolerant societies, too.

The problem of the parish community, both in its life and in its worship, is to maintain the balance between setting the highest ideals before its members with enthusiasm, and tolerating with love the mediocrity and mess of most of our lives. We have to have a real openness towards all men and women who make up the community, listening with love and humility and no patronizing 'tolerance'. At the same time we have to urge everyone forward with a certain authority and stretch him to his limits, because we must aim at the highest standards of discipleship. This is because we believe that God can make all of us saints, not just a few. Like St Benedict's Abbot in his Holy Rule, we have to lead in such a way that 'the strong may have something to strive after, and the weak nothing at which to take alarm' (ch. 64). In this, of all tasks, we can do nothing of ourselves but have to fall back on the strength of God's Spirit in us. It is frankly not possible out of one's own strength to walk this narrow way between arrogant enthusiasm which turns the timid away from Christ and tolerant mediocrity which inspires no one, so one is impelled to pray. Once again it is a case of the journey outwards being made possible only by the simultaneous journey into the heart of our being where the Holy Spirit dwells. There, if we let him, God gives us a new heart and enough wisdom and strength for every task he sets us. From that inspired centre we go out in his name to do 'all things', the all things St Paul promised us we could and would do because God gives us strength to do them. What we have to do is to let go sufficiently to allow that marvellous partnership to happen and then to set God free to flood our lives with his love and completely take us over.

Appendix

THE JOURNEY INWARDS:
A GUIDE FOR PRAYER

I sit before you, Lord, upright and relaxed, with a straight spine, allowing my weight to descend vertically through my body to the ground on which I am sitting.

I fix my mind within my body. I resist that urge of my mind to career out of the window to every other place but this one, and to career forwards and backwards in time away from the present. Gently and firmly I keep my mind where my body is : here, in this room.

In this present moment I let go all plans, worries, anxieties. I place them now in your hands, O Lord. I release my grip on them and allow you to take them over. For the moment I leave them to you.

I wait on you, passive and expectant.

You come towards me, and I let you carry me.

I begin the journey inwards. I travel down inside me to the inmost core of my being, where you dwell. In this deep centre of my being you are there before me, ceaselessly creating and energizing my whole person.

You, God are dynamic.

You are within me.

You are here.

You are now.

You are.

You are the ground of my being. I let go. I sink and merge into you. You overwhelm me. You flood my being. You take me over completely.

I let my breathing become this prayer of submission to you. My breathing, in and out, is the expression of my whole being.

I do it for you, with you, in you. I have 'become' you. You have 'become' me. We breathe together.

And now I open my eyes to see you in the world of things and people. I resume responsibility for my future. I take up again my plans, worries, anxieties. Renewed in strength I go again on the journey outwards, no longer alone, but in partnership with the Creator.

Prayer After Nine Rainy Days
by Pat Corrick Hinton
#8943 $2.95

Prayer Making
Discovering the Varieties of Prayer
by Richard W. Chilson
#8202 $5.95

Prayers for Growing and Other Pains
More Family Prayers
by Pat Corrick Hinton
#8193 $4.95

Praying
by Robert Faricy, S.J.
#8124 $3.50

The Breath of Life
A Simple Way to Pray
by Ron DelBene
with Herb Montgomery
#8180 $3.95

The Spirituality of John Henry Newman
by C. S. Dessain
#8173 $4.95

The Spirituality of Teilhard de Chardin
by Robert Faricy, S.J.
#8199 $5.95

The Way to Christianity
In Search of Spiritual Growth
Richard W. Chilson
#8111 $8.95

Available at your favorite bookstore or
directly from Winston Press, 430 Oak Grove,
Minneapolis, MN 55403.

John Dalrymple, an established
spiritual writer, is a parish priest in the
Archdiocese of Edinburgh. Before that
he served as spiritual director of a
seminary in Scotland and chaplain to
the students of St. Andrews University.